TOP
10
OF
IRELAND

TOP 10

OF
IRELAND

250 ESSENTIAL, AMUSING AND BIZARRE LISTS

EOGHAN CORRY
GENERAL EDITOR: RUSSELL ASH

hamlyn

An Hachette UK Company
www.hachette.co.uk

First published in Great Britain in 2010 by
Hamlyn, a division of Octopus Publishing Group Ltd
Endeavour House
189 Shaftesbury Avenue
London
WC2H 8JY
www.octopusbooks.co.uk

ISBN 978-0-600-62066-2

A CIP catalogue record for this book is available from the British Library.

Printed and bound in China.

10 9 8 7 6 5 4 3 2 1

Executive Editor: Trevor Davies
Editor: Ruth Wiseall
Executive Art Editor: Penny Stock
Designer: Sally Bond
Page make-up: Dorchester Typesetting Group Ltd
Senior Production Controller: Carolin Stransky

Artwork © Dover Books

CONTENTS

Introduction   13

What makes Ireland?   17
Top 10 highest mountains   18
Top 10 largest lakes   19
Top 10 longest rivers   20
Top 10 largest river catchments   21
Top 10 largest islands   22
Top 10 largest counties   23
Top 10 smallest counties   24
Top 10 most densely populated counties   25
Top 10 least densely populated counties   26
Top 10 counties with the highest male:female ratio   27
Top 10 counties with the highest female:male ratio   28
Top 10 counties with the highest percentage of early-risers   29
Top 10 counties with the highest percentage of long-distance
    commuters   30
Top 10 tallest structures   31
Top 10 tallest buildings   32
10 tallest features   33
Top 10 highest church spires   34

Living in Ireland   35
Top 10 populations in the Republic of Ireland   36
Top 10 most common surnames in the Republic of Ireland   37
Top 10 boys' names in the Republic of Ireland   38
Top 10 girls' names in the Republic of Ireland   39
Top 10 boys' names in Northern Ireland   40
Top 10 girls' names in Northern Ireland   41
Top 10 average prices for a three-bedroom house   42
Top 10 most expensive areas for a five-bedroom house in Dublin   43
Top 10 cheapest areas for a three-bedroom semi-detached house
    in Dublin   44

The 10 areas with the largest drop in asking house prices from
    peak levels   45
Top 10 wettest summers   46
Top 10 coldest winters   47
10 weather records   48
Top 10 nationalities living in the Republic of Ireland   49
Top 10 fastest-growing towns in the Republic of Ireland   50
Top 10 areas with the highest proportion of separated people   51
10 tips for a good relationship from Oscar Wilde   52
Top 10 means of travelling to work in the Republic of Ireland   53
10 of the worst times to have lived in Ireland   54
The 10 most commonly diagnosed cancers in the Republic of
    Ireland   56
Top 10 foreign languages used in courts in the Republic of
    Ireland   57
Top 10 most common crimes in the Republic of Ireland   58
The 10 most common causes of disputes in the Small Claims
    Court in the Republic of Ireland   59
10 defunct holidays   60
Top 10 fastest-growing religious affiliations in the Republic of
    Ireland   61
Top 10 largest religious affiliations   62
Top 10 largest religious affiliations in the Republic of Ireland   63
Top 10 smallest religious affiliations in the Republic of Ireland   64
Top 10 biggest lottery wins   65
10 things just as likely to happen as winning the Lotto jackpot   66
Top 10 most popular Leaving Cert subjects   67
The 10 least popular Leaving Cert subjects   68
Top 10 Leaving Cert subjects with the highest proportion of
    honours candidates   69
Top 10 Leaving Cert subjects with the highest proportion of
    A grades   70
The 10 most dangerous roads   71
The 10 worst years for deaths on the roads   72
Top 10 holiday destinations   73
Top 10 sun resorts visited   74

Ireland: A visitor's guide 75
Top 10 most popular visitor attractions 76
Top 10 most successful Tidy Towns 77
10 famous gardens 78
10 famous houses 79
10 famous castles 80
Top 10 most visited museums and galleries 81
Top 10 most visited castles and country houses 82
10 places on James Joyce's map of Dublin in *Ulysses* 83
Top 10 counties that attract the highest number of overseas
    visitors 84
10 views of the Irish 85
10 of the oldest pubs 86
10 places and the songs they inspired 88
Top 10 busiest airports 89
Top 10 destinations out of Dublin airport 90

Uniquely Irish 91
10 units of measurement 92
10 famous members of the Travelling community 94
10 riddles from the song tradition 95
10 fairy trees 96
10 *piseogs* 98
10 patron saints 99
10 bets placed with Paddy Power 100
10 iconic Irish pubs outside Ireland 101
10 counties and the food they are associated with 102
10 quintessential dishes 103
10 ways with a potato 104

The cultural isle 105
Top 10 bestselling fiction books 106
10 bestselling authors 107
10 novelists 108
10 20th-century novelists 110
10 playwrights 111
10 poets 112

10 travel writers 114
10 journalists 115
10 wonders of medieval Ireland according to Gerald of Wales 116
10 banned literary works 118
10 writers' pseudonyms 119
10 poets in the Irish language 120
10 writers of novels and memoirs in Irish 121
10 composers and musicians 122
Top 10 most expensive paintings by Irish artists 124
10 painters 125
10 ancient literary characters who may not have existed 126
10 hymns by Irish writers 128
10 philosophers 130

Entertainment 131
10 entertainers you might not recognize 132
10 traditional singers 133
10 traditional musicians 134
10 famous melodies 136
10 modern songwriters 137
10 phrases you'll need to write your own Irish ballad 138
10 Oscar winners 139
10 film actors 140
10 stage stars 141
10 comedians 142
10 film directors 143
Top 10 best films 144
10 movies filmed in Ireland 145
10 banned movies 146
Top 10 TV programmes 147
10 quotes from *Father Ted* 148
10 references in *The Simpsons* 149
10 famous advertising campaigns 150
The 10 first programmes shown on RTÉ 151
10 firsts for Irish radio 152

Words and language 153
10 words invented in Ireland 154
10 phrases from the Irish language 155
10 English words derived from the Irish language 156
10 words in Ulster Scots 157
10 words in Shelta 158
10 words in Yola 159
10 phrases in Yola 160

The famous and infamous 161
10 Oscar Wilde one-liners 162
10 famous people and the ages at which they died 163
10 people awarded the freedom of Dublin 164
10 Nobel Laureates 165
10 aviators 166
10 surprising birthplaces 167
10 honorary citizens 168
10 notable centenarians 169
10 men behind the initials 170
10 famous people who left school early 171
10 tales of sexual exploits 172
10 Irishmen who never married 174
10 people from large families 175
10 people who studied in Ireland 176
10 people with an Irish father 177
10 people with an Irish mother 178
10 people with an Irish grandfather 179
10 people with an Irish grandmother 180
Top 10 wealthiest people 181
Top 10 wealthiest people in 2001 182

The historic isle 183
10 dogs 184
10 high kings 186
10 things that happened in 1916 apart from the Rising 187
10 sieges 188
The 10 most costly conflicts 189

10 famous people (9 military and 1 bishop) who changed sides   190
10 great battles   192
10 military commanders   194
The 10 worst disasters   195
10 master mariners   196
10 shipwrecks   197
10 highwaymen   198
10 places where public executions took place   199
10 execution milestones   200
10 events that occurred on Friday 13th   201
10 unusual burial places of historical figures   202
10 gods from Celtic mythology   203
10 goddesses from Celtic mythology   204
10 saints of early Ireland   205
10 religious founders   206
10 religious controversies   207
10 people who changed religion   208
Top 10 countries and their Irish diaspora   209
10 philanthropists and campaigners   210
10 medical pioneers   211
10 engineers   212
10 inventors   213
10 mathematicians   214
10 physicists   215
10 biologists   216
10 chemists   217
10 explorers   218

Trade and industry   219
10 architects   220
10 fashion designers   222
Top 10 most-caught fish   223
Top 10 highest trade surpluses   224
Top 10 export markets   225
Top 10 import sources   226
Top 10 facts about the Republic of Ireland's place in Europe   227
Top 10 bestselling makes of car in the Republic of Ireland   228

Top 10 largest trade unions   229
Top 10 smallest trade unions   230
Top 10 largest companies in 1885   231
Top 10 largest companies in 1975   232
Top 10 largest companies in 1980   233
Top 10 largest companies in 2008   234
Top 10 largest retailers   235
10 famous exports   236
Top 10 largest financial houses   238

Politics and politicians   239
10 close election calls   240
Top 10 biggest vote-getters in Dáil elections   242
10 groundbreaking female leaders   243
Top 10 shortest budget speeches   244
Top 10 longest budget speeches   245
10 famous political nicknames   246
10 referendum results   247
10 Supreme Court decisions   248
10 tribunals of inquiry   249
10 famous members of the 18th-century Irish Parliament   250
10 parliamentary constituencies in Grattan's time   252
10 people who might have shot Michael Collins   253
10 Irish-born prime ministers of other states/countries   254

The sporting isle   255
10 world champions   256
10 forgotten world champions   257
10 Olympic stories   258
10 Summer Olympics near misses   260
Top 10 greatest ever sportspeople   261
10 record-breaking years for athletics   262
10 grand dams of racing   264
10 Aintree winners   265
10 Cheltenham heroes   266
10 champion trainers   268
10 champion jockeys   270

10 flat champion horses   271
10 sporting controversies   272
10 sporting disasters   274
10 record sports attendances   276
Top 10 players with the most rugby caps   277
10 national rugby victories   278
10 showjumping stories   279
10 signature golf holes   280
10 golfers   281
10 members of the International Boxing Hall of Fame   282
10 world boxing champions   283
10 Olympic boxing medallists   284
10 famous GAA sagas   285
10 memorable football scores   286
10 memorable hurling scores   287
Top 10 counties ranked by GAA clubs   288
Top 10 most successful GAA counties   289
Top 10 players with the most All Star awards in hurling   290
10 soccer clubs with Irish names   291
10 Republic of Ireland soccer players who were born in England   292
10 soccer stars   293
10 great years for the IFA   294
10 great years for the FAI   295
Top 10 most-capped Republic of Ireland players   296
Top 10 most-capped Northern Ireland players   297
10 soccer clubs in Europe   298
10 foreign internationals who played in the Irish soccer leagues   299
10 goalkeepers who have scored goals   300
10 hockey milestones   301
10 great years for cricket   302
10 men who played more than one sport for Ireland   303

Acknowledgements   304

INTRODUCTION

INTRODUCTION

'The luck of the Irish'

Being Irish can be a question of location, birth, domicile, ancestry or profession. This makes compiling the *Top 10 of Ireland* a challenging and richly rewarding exercise. It also means that a Top 10 of Ireland is, of necessity, a very inclusive thing, extending beyond the shores of Ireland itself. Someone from Brooklyn or Brisbane with an Irish grandfather, might find their way into this book, as would a place name in America or even someone who stopped by for a weekend and found a home here. This wide-ranging influence across the world has been defined by the high rate of emigration during the colonial and immediate post-colonial period. The first waves of emigrants fled to France and Spain to escape religious and political persecution in the 17th and 18th centuries. Later, emigrants went to America, the Antipodes and Britain. Their descendants form the Irish diaspora that dwarfes the population of the island today, headed by the 44 million people in the USA who claim Irish ancestry, some through five and six generations. The population of Ireland itself is now creeping towards 6.5 million, after 150 years of near continuous decline, and is spread through about 3,000 separate communities, increasingly urban in nature, each with stories to tell.

The Emerald Isle

The island itself is compact and complex. The stats are easily remembered by school children: 32,000 square miles in 32 counties; 20th largest island in the world and almost exactly the same size as Austria, Maine or, indeed, Lake Superior. The mild and damp weather is dictated by an annual arm-wrestling match between the Icelandic low and the Azores high weather systems, giving rise to the famously unpredictable cloud patterns. The continuous supply of light rain keeps the country green, which gives it its soubriquet 'the Emerald Isle'. The landscape, celebrated in the lists that follow, resembles a dinner plate, with the mountains rimmed around the coastline, and the rivers, mainly the Shannon, draining the interior. The analogy goes further. The produce of this interior fills the dinner plates of Europe and it is no surprise that Ireland's population is outnumbered by the farm animals they raise. The economy, which over-performed in the agricultural age and then under-performed in the Industrial Revolution, is driven today by the knowledge economy, a workforce with a high standard of education and the trappings of technology.

The gift of the gab

Ireland's international reach is reinforced by the country's worldwide impact in the fields of literature and music. The traditional Irish language, Gaelic, is largely a cultural artefact, spoken by about 20 per cent of the population, so the rhythms and nuances of the native tongue are conveyed instead in English. Some say that this way with words and the charming lilt of an Irish accent is a factor in the large number of Irish writers of songs and stories who have found fame in the Anglophone world. Some of our lists have attempted to reflect that, but by necessity they are based on peer-accolade and marketplace sales rather than on any more precise measurement.

What's in a name?

Ireland is the name of the island and, confusingly, the state, under the 1937 constitution. The Greeks preferred 'Juverna', and Caesar used 'Hibernia', perhaps confused with the word for winter, *hibernus*, to create the oft-quoted 'winter island'. Ptolemy called it 'Iouernia', in his map of AD 150 and the people, known as the Scotti, were to give their name to Ireland's nearest neighbour, Scotland. It was from Éirinn that the current English-language name of Ireland derived in the 12th century, to which was added the Germanic 'land'. Ériu, Banba and Fódhla were the three mythological goddesses who asked that the country be named for them. An oft-quoted passage in the *Book of Invasions*, *Lebor Gabála Érenn*, tells how Ériu prevailed. The Irish-language name for the island and state, Éire, is sometimes used by historians to refer to the 26-county unit that existed between the end of the Irish Free State in 1937 and the declaration of the Republic in 1949. The technically inaccurate Republic of Ireland, which is not recorded in any official document, is the term used by FIFA, the ruling body of association football, the only major sport to which partition applies. 'Southern Ireland', also sometimes pejoratively used to describe the state, existed for a day under English law on 28 June 1921. 'Northern Ireland', a name created at the same time, however, endured as the official name for the north-eastern counties, still subject to rule by Westminster after partition in 1921.

Sorting fact from fiction

The island's history is relatively easy to research. An island off the European mainland is always in danger of being marginalized, so ancient Ireland turned to the bards and historians to assure its place in literary and popular culture. The medieval literature of Ireland is embedded with facts, genealogies, lists and superlatives, founded in folklore but stated with the confidence that years of working with a quill pen can bestow. Exact dates were accorded to mythical events, the Battle of Moytura, the foundation of the House of Tara, the life of St Patrick and the 300 kings of Tara who preceded the first historical ones, family trees compiled that went back to Noah and detailed accounts given of seven mythical invasions.

Conquest meant that the new owners had to measure the extent of the land they had taken. The first maps and the population statistics of the 17th century were, at best, elaborate guesswork. The appetite for compiling statistics began with the French Revolution and the emergence of centrally organized Napoleonic states. Ireland's British rulers caught the bug in the early 19th century, and by the 1840s statistical surveys had been completed to ascertain the height, area and population of every parish. When there were taxes to collect, we learned how many windows there were in Ireland. We know more about the genealogy of 18th-century racehorses than we know about 18th-century people. Today's surveys are based on different criteria. Businesses are rated by turnover, not rateable valuation. The 1841 census will tell you there were 91 shipwrights in Co. Wexford; that of 2006 will tell you how long people in the county will take to commute to work.

The story behind the figures

A Top 10 list will always be at the mercy of the sources and statistics it is based on. Multipliers and representative samples are the enemy of the statistician. Websites use inconsistent tracking devices to verify the information they record. Researchers with clipboards extrapolate that everyone they interview represents a sizeable slice of the population they have not interviewed. Even major census returns reflect activity on one night every five years and can be distorted by events such as a rock concert or a sporting fixture. Nonetheless, a Top 10 will give a taste for something larger, the real story behind the list.

The real story of Ireland is somewhat more elusive, something that is always worth taking the time to explore. We hope you enjoy the journey.

WHAT MAKES
IRELAND?

HIGHEST MOUNTAINS

	Mountain	Height
1	Carrauntoohil, Co. Kerry	1, 039 m (3,409 ft)
2	Knocknapeasta, Co. Kerry	988 m (3,241 ft)
3	Brandon, Co. Kerry	951 m (3,123 ft)
4	Lugnaquilla, Co. Wicklow	924 m (3,035 ft)
5	Galtymore, Co. Limerick/Co. Tipperary	917 m (3,015 ft)
6	Baurtregaum, Co. Kerry	851 m (2,796 ft)
7	Slieve Donard, Co. Down	850 m (2,792 ft)
8	Mullaghcleevaun, Co. Wicklow	849 m (2,786 ft)
9	Skregmore, Co. Kerry	848 m (2,784 ft)
10	Brandon Peak, Co. Kerry	842 m (2,764 ft)

Three other peaks of over 914 m (3,000 feet) form part of the Carrauntoohil ridge: Beenkeragh (1,010 m/3,314 ft), Caher (975 m/3,200 ft) and a third unnamed peak (957m/3,141 ft), while there are also three on the 6-mile (10-km) ridge on top of Brandon, one unnamed (933 m/3,062 ft) and Brandon Peak. An unnamed peak near Mullaghcleevaun rises to 846 m (2,776 ft). The claim of the highest cliffs in Ireland (and third-highest sea cliffs in Europe) is held by Slieve League at 668 m (2,191 ft).

LARGEST LAKES

	Lake	County	Area
1	Lough Neagh	Antrim, Armagh, Derry and Tyrone	383 sq km (148 sq miles)
2	Lough Corrib	Galway	175 sq km (67 sq miles)
3	Lough Derg	Tipperary, Galway, Clare	118 sq km (46 sq miles)
4	Lough Erne Lower	Fermanagh	111 sq km (43 sq miles)
5	Lough Ree	Longford, Westmeath, Roscommon	105 sq km (41 sq miles)
6	Lough Mask	Mayo	89 sq km (34 sq miles)
7	Lough Conn	Mayo	57 sq km (22 sq miles)
8	Lough Allen	Leitrim	35 sq km (14 sq miles)
9	Lough Erne Upper	Fermanagh	34.5 sq km (13 sq miles)
10	Poulaphouca	Kerry	12 sq km (5 sq miles)

Poulaphouca is Ireland's largest man-made lake.

LONGEST RIVERS

1   **Shannon 386 km (240 miles)**
    Path: near Dowra in Cavan through Lough Allen, Lough Ree and Lough Derg to tidal waters at Limerick. It is an important artery for river traffic and power supply.

2   **Barrow 192 km (120 miles)**
    Path: Glenbarrow in the Slieve Bloom Mountains, Co. Laois, to tidal waters near New Ross.

3   **Suir 184 km (114 miles)**
    Path: Devil's Bit Mountain, Co. Tipperary, to Waterford City.

4   **Munster Blackwater 168 km (104 miles)**
    Path: Mullaghareirk Mountains, Co. Kerry, through north Cork to Youghal.

5   **Nore 140 km (87 miles)**
    Path: Devil's Bit Mountain, Co. Tipperary, through Kilkenny to Waterford City.

6   **Bann 129 km (80 miles)**
    Path: Slieve Muck in the Mourne Mountains through Lough Neagh to Portstewart.

7   **Liffey 125 km (78 miles)**
    Path: Kippure, Co. Wicklow, in a semicircle through Co. Kildare and through Dublin City.

8   **Slaney 117 km (73 miles)**
    Path: Lugnaquilla, Co. Wicklow, to Wexford Town.

9   **Boyne 112 km (70 miles)**
    Path: Carbury, Co. Kildare, past the heritage sites of Co. Meath to Drogheda.

10 **Erne 105 km (64 miles)**
    Path: Beaghy Lough, near Stradone, Co. Cavan, through Lough Gowna, Lough Oughter and Upper and Lower Lough Erne in Co. Fermanagh to Ballyshannon, Co. Donegal.

LARGEST RIVER CATCHMENTS

	River	Area
1	Shannon	15,700 sq km (6,016 sq miles)
2	Bann	5,810 sq km (2,243 sq miles)
3	Erne	4,370 sq km (1,687 sq miles)
4	Suir	3,610 sq km (1,394 sq miles)
5	Munster Blackwater	3,330 sq km (1,286 sq miles)
6	Corrib	3,140 sq km (1,212 sq miles)
7	Barrow	3,070 sq km (1,185 sq miles)
8	Foyle	2,920 sq km (1,127 sq miles)
9	Boyne	2,700 sq km (1,042 sq miles)
10	Nore	2,530 sq km (977 sq miles)

The Shannon basin includes large areas of counties Limerick, Clare, north Tipperary, Offaly, Westmeath, Longford and Roscommon, significant parts of counties Kerry, Galway, Leitrim and Cavan, and smaller parts of Fermanagh, Sligo, south Tipperary, Mayo, Cork, Laois and Meath.

TOP 10

LARGEST ISLANDS

	Island	Area
1	Achill	14,669 ha (36,248 acres)
2	Inish Mór	3,090 ha (7,635 acres)
3	Valentia	2,632 ha (6,504 acres)
4	Gorumna	2,391 ha (5,908 acres)
5	Bere	1,773 ha (4,381 acres)
6	Arranmore	1,763 ha (4,356 acres)
7	Clear Island	1,632 ha (4,033 acres)
8	Clare Island	1,628 ha (4,024 acres)
9	Rathlin	1,442 ha (3,564 acres)
10	Lettermore	912 ha (2,253 acres)

Ireland has 348 offshore islands, 117 of them in Clew Bay, and 181 inland islands situated on lakes.

TOP 10

LARGEST COUNTIES

County	Area
1 Cork	7,459 sq km (2,880 sq miles)
2 Galway	5,939 sq km (2,293 sq miles)
3 Mayo	5,398 sq km (2,084 sq miles)
4 Donegal	4,830 sq km (1,865 sq miles)
5 Kerry	4,701 sq km (1,815 sq miles)
6 Tipperary	4,255 sq km (1,643 sq miles)
7 Tyrone	3,263 sq km (1,220 sq miles)
8 Clare	3,188 sq km (1,231 sq miles)
9 Antrim	2,838 sq km (1,092 sq miles)
10 Limerick	2,686 sq km (1,038 sq miles)

TOP 10
SMALLEST COUNTIES

	County	Area
1	Louth	821 sq km (317 sq miles)
2	Carlow	896 sq km (346 sq miles)
3	Dublin	922 sq km (356 sq miles)
4	Longford	1,044 sq km (403 sq miles)
5	Armagh	1,253 sq km (484 sq miles)
6	Monaghan	1,291 sq km (498 sq miles)
7	Leitrim	1,525 sq km (589 sq miles)
8	Fermanagh	1,678 sq km (648 sq miles)
9	Kildare	1,694 sq km (654 sq miles)
10	Laois	1,719 sq km (664 sq miles)

MOST DENSELY
POPULATED COUNTIES

	County	People per sq km*
1	Dublin	1,287
2	Antrim	216
3	Down	167
4	Louth	136
5	Derry	112
6	Kildare	110
7	Armagh	101
8	Wexford	74
9	Meath	69
10	Limerick	68

* Based on the 2006 Census; totals for Northern Ireland based on the 2004 figures
Source: Central Statistics Office Ireland and www.nisra.gov.uk

TOP 10

LEAST DENSELY POPULATED COUNTIES

	County	People per sq km*
1	Leitrim	19
2=	Mayo	23
=	Roscommon	23
4=	Kerry	30
=	Donegal	30
6	Sligo	33
=	Longford	33
=	Cavan	33
9=	Fermanagh	34
=	Clare	34

* Based on the 2006 Census; totals for Northern Ireland based on the 2004 figures
Source: Central Statistics Office Ireland and www.nisra.gov.uk

COUNTIES WITH THE HIGHEST MALE:FEMALE RATIO

	County	Ratio*
1	Leitrim	1,061:1,000
2	Cavan	1,059:1,000
3	Roscommon	1,056:1,000
4	Laois	1,054:1,000
5	Longford	1,045:1,000
6	Monaghan	1,043:1,000
7	Carlow	1,035:1,000
8	Meath	1,031:1,000
9	Offaly	1,029:1,000
10	Tipperary	1,028:1,000

* Based on the 2006 Census
Source: Central Statistics Office Ireland

TOP 10
COUNTIES WITH THE HIGHEST FEMALE:MALE RATIO

	County	Ratio*
1	Dublin	1,037:1,000
2	Sligo	1,013:1,000
3	Louth	1,011:1,000
4	Wicklow	1,006:1,000
5	Cork	999:1,000
6	Wexford	994:1,000
7	Westmeath	993:1,000
8	Donegal	991:1,000
9	Galway	989:1,000
10	Limerick	986:1,000

* Based on the 2006 Census
Source: Central Statistics Office Ireland

TOP 10
COUNTIES WITH THE HIGHEST PERCENTAGE OF EARLY-RISERS*

	County	Percentage of workforce
1	Dublin	30.21
2	Kildare	8.27
3	Meath	8.15
4	Cork	7.99
5	Galway	3.70
6	Wicklow	3.64
7	Louth	3.52
8	Wexford	3.33
9	Tipperary	3.07
10	Limerick	2.91

* People who leave for work before 6.30 a.m., based on the 2006 Census
Source: Central Statistics Office Ireland

TOP 10

COUNTIES WITH THE HIGHEST PERCENTAGE OF LONG-DISTANCE COMMUTERS*

	County	Percentage of workforce
1	Dublin	24.83
2	Meath	11.49
3	Kildare	10.97
4	Wicklow	4.92
5	Louth	4.31
6	Cork	4.10
7	Laois	3.77
8	Wexford	3.72
9	Westmeath	3.39
10	Galway	3.11

* People who have more than a 1½-hour commute to work, based on the 2006 Census
Source: Central Statistics Office Ireland

TALLEST STRUCTURES

	Structure/location	Opened	Height
1	UHF/VHF transmitter, Strabane	1963	305.5 m (1,002 ft)
2	Medium wave transmitter, Tullamore	1975	290 m (951 ft)
3	Long wave transmitter, Clarkstown	1988	245 m (804 ft)
4	Power station chimneys, Moneypoint	1987	218 m (715 ft)
5	Power station chimneys, Poolbeg	1971	207.8 m (682 ft)
6	Power station chimneys, Kilroot	1977	198 m (650 ft)
7	RTÉ FM/TV transmitter, Mullaghanish	1962	152 m (499 ft)
8	Power station chimneys, Tarbert	1969	151 m (495 ft)
9	Lisnagarvey radio mast, Sprucefield	1936	145 m (475 ft)
10	Power station chimneys, Great Island	1968	138 m (453 ft)

TOP 10

TALLEST BUILDINGS

	Building/location	Height	Opened
1	Obel Tower, Belfast	85 m (279 ft)	2010
2	Windsor House, Belfast	80 m (262 ft)	1975
3	Belfast City Hospital Tower, Belfast	74 m (243 ft)	1986
4	The Elysian, Cork	71 m (233 ft)	2008
5	County Hall, Cork	67 m (220 ft)	1968
6	Hilton Hotel, Belfast	63 m (207 ft)	1998
=	Millennium Tower, Dublin	63 m (207 ft)	1998
8	BT Riverside Tower, Belfast	62 m (203 ft)	1997
9	Divis Tower, Belfast	61 m (200 ft)	1966
10	Liberty Hall, Dublin	59.4 m (195 ft)	1965

The Elysian in Cork has a spire that takes the building's total height to 81 m (266 ft).

TALLEST FEATURES 10

	Feature	Location	Opened	Height
1	Tallest bridge: River Suir Bridge	Waterford	2009	100 m (330 ft)
2	Tallest castle: Nenagh	Nenagh	c.1220	31 m (102 ft)
3	Tallest gantry crane: Samson, Harland and Wolff	Belfast	1974	106 m (348 ft)
4	Tallest lighthouse: Fastnet	Off coast of Co. Cork	1904	54 m (177 ft)
5	Tallest moving sculpture: Irish Wave	Park West, Dublin	2001	35.4 m (116 ft)
6	Tallest obelisk: Wellington Monument	Phoenix Park, Dublin	1861	63 m (207 ft)
7	Tallest round tower: Kilmacduagh Monastery	Near Gort	c.1100	34 m (112 ft)
8	Tallest sculpture: Spire of Dublin	Dublin	2003	120 m (394 ft)
9	Tallest standing stone: Punchestown	Co. Kildare	2400–1800 BC	6.5 m (21 ft)
10	Tallest windmill: Kilgarvan Wind Farm	Kilgarvan	2005	93 m (305 ft)

HIGHEST CHURCH SPIRES

	Church/location	Opened	Height
1	St John's Cathedral, Limerick	1861	93.8 m (308 ft)
2	St Colman's Cathedral, Cobh	1915	91.4 m (300 ft)
3	St Mary's Cathedral, Killarney	1912	86.8 m (285 ft)
4	St Patrick's Church, Maynooth	1891	83 m (272 ft)
5	St Eugene's Cathedral, Derry	1873	78 m (256 ft)
6	St Macartan's Cathedral, Monaghan	1892	74.6 m (245 ft)
7=	St Finbarre's Cathedral, Cork	1879	73 m (240 ft)
=	Cathedral of St Eunan and St Colmcille, Letterkenny	1901	73 m (240 ft)
9	Church of SS Augustine and John, Dublin	1874	70 m (230 ft)
10	Pro-Cathedral of St Peter and St Paul, Ennis	1735	69 m (226 ft)

LIVING IN IRELAND

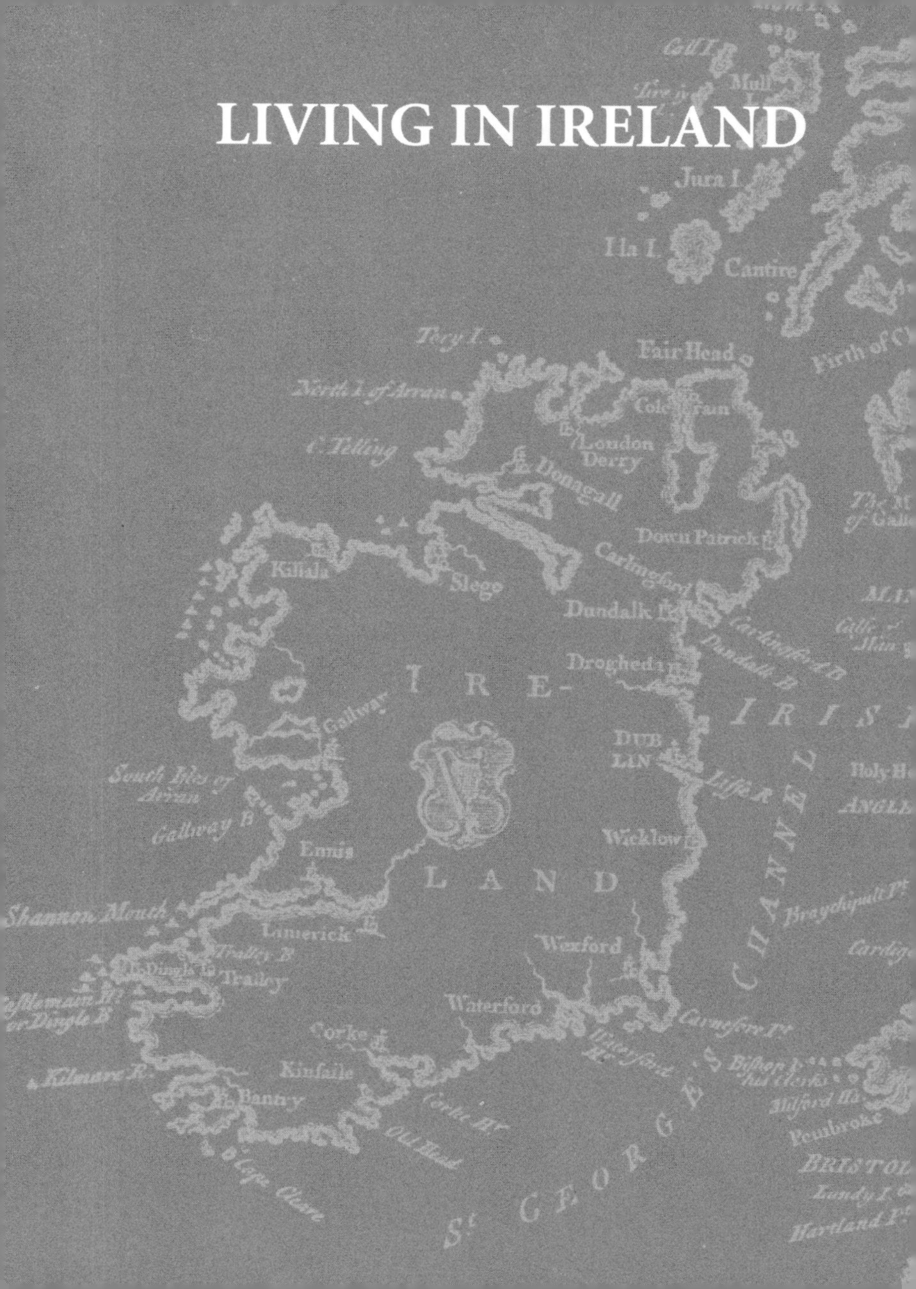

TOP 10

POPULATIONS
in the Republic of Ireland

	Population	Number*
1	Chickens	12.7 million
2	Cattle	6.7 million
3	Sheep	5.5 million
4	People	4.4 million
5	Pigs	1.6 million
6	Other poultry	1.2 million
7	Horses and ponies	89,000
8	Deer	9,600
9	Goats	7,300
10	Donkeys	7,200

* Figures for 2007
Source: Central Statistics Office Ireland

MOST COMMON SURNAMES
in the Republic of Ireland

1 Murphy

2 O'Connor

3 Kelly

4 O'Brien

5 Ryan

6 Walsh

7 Byrne

8 O'Sullivan

9 McCarthy

10 O'Neill

TOP 10

BOYS' NAMES
in the Republic of Ireland*

1 Jack

2 Sean

3 Conor

4 Daniel

5 James

6 Ryan

7 Adam

8 Dylan

9 Luke

10 Alex

* In 2008
Source: Central Statistics Office Ireland

TOP 10

GIRLS' NAMES
in the Republic of Ireland*

1   Ava

2   Katie

3   Sarah

4   Emma

5   Emily

6   Sophie

7   Grace

8   Aoife

9   Chloe

10 Kate

* In 2008
Source: Central Statistics Office Ireland

TOP 10
BOYS' NAMES
in Northern Ireland*

1   Jack

2   Matthew

3   Daniel

4   James

5   Ryan

6   Adam

7   Ethan

8   Charlie

9   Thomas

10 Conor

* In 2009
Source: NI Census Office

TOP 10

GIRLS' NAMES
in Northern Ireland*

1   Katie

2   Sophie

3   Grace

4   Lucy

5   Erin

6   Emily

7   Emma

8   Eva

9   Chloe

10 Anna

* In 2009
Source: NI Census Office

TOP 10

AVERAGE PRICES FOR A THREE-BEDROOM HOUSE

	Area	Q3 2009 (€)	Q4 2009 (€)
1	South Dublin City	386,000	353,000
2	South Co. Dublin	346,000	337,000
3	North Dublin City	331,000	313,000
4	Co. Wicklow	318,000	309,000
5	Dublin City Centre	326,000	306,000
6	North Co. Dublin	298,000	293,000
7	West Co. Dublin	275,000	259,000
8=	Cork City	263,000	243,000
=	Co. Kildare	246,000	243,000
10	Galway City	257,000	242,000

Source: www.daft.ie

MOST EXPENSIVE AREAS FOR A
FIVE-BEDROOM HOUSE
in Dublin

	Area	Price (€)*
1	Foxrock	2,295,663
2	Dalkey	2,079,270
3	Howth	1,755,172
4	Booterstown	1,691,550
5	Blackrock	1,633,282
6	Rathgar	1,587,667
7	Ranelagh	1,586,924
8	Monkstown	1,572,414
9	Killiney	1,547,763
10	Dún Laoghaire	1,527,805

* Figures at peak for Q4 2006
Source: www.daft.ie

CHEAPEST AREAS FOR A THREE-BEDROOM SEMI-DETACHED HOUSE
in Dublin

	Area	Price (€)*
1	Newcastle	331,990
2	Balbriggan	340,322
3	Mulhuddart	342,433
4	Cherry Orchard/Park West	346,545
5	Tyrelstown	357,258
6	Poppintree	360,379
7	Clondalkin	362,845
8	Maynooth	363,210
9	Leixlip	370,062
10	Celbridge	375,183

* Figures at peak for Q4 2006
Source: www.daft.ie

THE 10
AREAS WITH THE LARGEST DROP IN HOUSE PRICES FROM PEAK LEVELS

	Area	Average price (€)*	Percentage drop
1	Dublin City Centre	245,352	42.7
2	Louth	209,168	38.3
3	South Co. Dublin	427,903	37.2
4	Westmeath	182,298	36.8
5	South Dublin City	298,629	36.4
6	Longford	149,098	36.3
7=	Monaghan	204,950	35.8
=	Offaly	192,561	35.8
9	West Co. Dublin	232,722	35.3
10	Wexford	207,143	34.6

* Figures for Q4 2009
Source: www.daft.ie

According to the National House Prices Survey by www.daft.ie, asking prices were down 19 per cent on average in 2009 following a decrease of almost 15 per cent in 2008. At the end of the final quarter of 2009 prices dropped to just over €242,000, €110,000 below their peak.

WETTEST SUMMERS

	Year	Rainfall*
1	1879	Fig. not available
2	1958	426.4 cm (167 in)
3	2007	391.8 cm (154 in)
4	2008	377.7 cm (148½ in)
5	1900	367.3 cm (144½ in)
6	1986	316.8 cm (124½ in)
7	1895	315.6 cm (124 in)
8	2009	309.2 cm (122 in)
9	1912	308.6 cm (121½ in)
10	1985	304.5 cm (120 in)

* Data for accumulated June, July and August rainfall, collected in Dublin

1879 is the wettest summer on record. Between March and September it rained on 125 out of 183 days.

TOP 10
COLDEST WINTERS

1   1895

2   1947

3   1881

4   1963

5   1917

6   1955

7   1892

8   1886

9   1900

10 1941

The winters of 1814, 1947 and 1963 were noted for their snowfall.

10 WEATHER RECORDS

	Record	Place	Date
1	Highest air temperature: 33.3°C (91.94°F)	Kilkenny Castle	26 Jun 1887
2	Highest air temperature in 20th century: 32.5°C (90.5°F)	Boora, Co. Offaly	29 Jun 1976
3	Lowest air temperature: 19.1°C (66.38°F)	Markree Castle, Co. Sligo	16 Jan 1881
4	Lowest grass temperature: -19.6°C (-3.28°F)	Glasnevin, Dublin	12 Jan 1982
5	Driest year: 356.6 mm (14 in) of rain	Glasnevin, Dublin	1887
6	Longest drought: 38 days	Limerick	3 Apr–10 May 1938
7	Monthly rainfall: 790 mm (31.1 in)	Comeragh Mountains, Co. Waterford	Oct 1996
8	Annual rainfall: 3,964.9 mm (156 in)	Ballaghbeama Gap, Co. Kerry	1960
9	Hourly rainfall: 97 mm (3.81 in)	Orra Beg, Co. Antrim	Aug 1980
10	Daily rainfall: 243.5 mm (9.59 in)	Cloone Lake, Co. Kerry	18 Sept 1993

Source: Meteorological Service

TOP 10
NATIONALITIES LIVING
in the Republic of Ireland

	Nationality	Number of people*
1	English/Welsh	204,746
2	Polish	63,090
3	American	25,181
4	Lithuanian	24,808
5	Scottish	16,863
6	Nigerian	16,677
7	Latvian	13,999
8	German	11,797
9	Chinese	11,218
10	Filipino	9,644

* Based on the 2006 Census
Source: Central Statistics Office Ireland

TOP 10

FASTEST-GROWING TOWNS
in the Republic of Ireland

	Town	Percentage*
1	Balbriggan	+51.1
2	Navan	+28.0
3	Midleton	+26.3
4	Swords	+25.1
5	Greystones	+22.3
6	Portlaoise	+20.5
7	Mullingar	+17.9
8	Tullamore	+16.5
9	Letterkenny	+15.5
10	Cobh	+15.2

* Percentage rise in population between 2002 and 2006, based on 2006 Census
Source: Central Statistics Office Ireland

TOP 10
AREAS WITH THE HIGHEST PROPORTION OF SEPARATED PEOPLE

	Area	Percentage*
1	Dublin	30.52
2	Cork	10.47
3	Limerick	4.49
4	Wexford	4.48
5	Kildare	4.39
6	Galway	4.37
7	Meath	3.78
8	Wicklow	3.48
9	Louth	3.24
10	Donegal	3.20

* Based on the 2006 Census as a percentage of the national total
Source: Central Statistics Office Ireland

10
TIPS FOR A GOOD RELATIONSHIP FROM OSCAR WILDE

1   'A man can be happy with any woman as long as he does not love her.'

2   'Men marry because they are tired, women because they are curious; both are disappointed.'

3   'Modern women understand everything except their husbands.'

4   'No man should keep a secret from his wife, she invariably finds it out.'

5   'One can always recognize women who trust their husbands, they look so thoroughly unhappy.'

6   'One should always be in love; that is the reason one should never marry.'

7   'The book of life begins with a man and a woman in a garden, and it ends with Revelations.'

8   'The one charm of marriage is that it makes a life of deception absolutely necessary for both parties.'

9   'The proper basis for marriage is a mutual misunderstanding.'

10 'There's nothing in the world like the devotion of a married woman, it's the thing no married man knows anything about.'

MEANS OF TRAVELLING TO WORK
in the Republic of Ireland

	Form of transport	Percentage	Number of people*
1	Motor car – driver	57.08	1,080,446
2	On foot	10.87	205,688
3	Lorry or van	7.77	147,035
4	Bus	6.07	114,956
5	Work at home	5.58	105,706
6	Motor car – passenger	5.54	104,861
7	Train (DART or LUAS)	2.90	54,942
8	Bicycle	1.90	36,306
9	Not stated	1.57	29,798
10	Motorcycle	0.69	13,049

* Based on the 2006 Census
Source: Central Statistics Office Ireland

10 OF THE WORST TIMES TO HAVE LIVED IN IRELAND

1   **795**
    On 8 June, Vikings made their first attack on Ireland, sacking Rathlin Island. During the next 25 years there was, on average, one Viking attack per year.

2   **1348–9**
    The Black Death arrived in Ireland via ships landing at the ports of Drogheda and Howth in the summer of 1348. By Christmas 1348, 14,000 had died in Dublin, according to Kilkenny-based Franciscan friar John Clyn.

3   **1581–2**
    Scorched-earth warfare in Munster killed 30,000.

4   **1649–70**
    Scorched-earth warfare and the plague caused the population to reduce from 2.1 million to 1.7 million.

5   **1740**
    Icebergs appeared off the Irish coast in the coldest winter to strike Ireland since records began. Many died of the cold or the famine that followed, which wiped out an estimated 400,000 (about one-eighth of the population).

6   **1817–19**
    Famine and typhus killed around 50,000.

7   **1832**
    Around 25,000 died in the first of four cholera epidemics. As many as 35,000 died in 1848–50. There were further cholera epidemics in 1853–4, and 1866–7.

8   **1845–9**
    The potato crop was ruined three times in five years by *Phytophthora infestans*, commonly called potato blight. It was first noticed in August 1845. Over 3 million people were totally dependent upon potatoes for food. By the time it had abated an estimated 1 million people died. Another million emigrated to the USA and other countries. A sixth of all travellers on the ships died en route of typhus or cholera.

9   1918

Between the end of the First World War and the outbreak of the War of Independence early in 1919, Ireland was hit by an influenza pandemic in which 20,000 died (this is more deaths than those caused by the War of Independence and Civil War combined). It began in March 1918, came in three waves and spread rapidly as a result of the post-war movements of troops and refugees.

10   1941

In April–May 1941, Belfast suffered two major German air raids in which over 1,000 people perished. In all some 56,000 houses – over half the city's total housing stock – were damaged.

MOST COMMONLY DIAGNOSED CANCERS in the Republic of Ireland

	Type of cancer	Number of cases*
1	Non-melanoma	7,076
2	Prostate	2,536
3	Breast	2,479
4	Colorectal	2,174
5	Lung	1,742
6	Melanoma	667
7	Lymphoma	646
8	Bladder	478
9	Stomach	455
10	Oesophagus	402

*Figures for 2007
Source: Central Statistics Office Ireland

FOREIGN LANGUAGES
USED IN COURTS
in the Republic of Ireland*

1 Polish

2 Romanian

3 Lithuanian

4 Russian

5 Mandarin Chinese

6 Latvian

7 Portuguese

8 French

9 Czech

10 Arabic

* In 2008
Source: Courts Service of Ireland

MOST COMMON CRIMES
in the Republic of Ireland

	Crime	Cases reported*
1	Speeding (driving)	199,030
2	Theft and related offences	76,796
3	Public order	61,919
4	Damage to property	44,797
5	Mobile phone usage while driving	32,672
6	Not wearing a seatbelt while driving	30,459
7	Burglary	24,707
8	Controlled drug offences	23,422
9	Dangerous and negligent acts (including driving while drunk)	19,613
10	Threats, assaults and harassment	19,254

* Figures for 2008
Source: An Garda Siochana

MOST COMMON CAUSES OF DISPUTES IN THE SMALL CLAIMS COURT
in the Republic of Ireland

1   Holidays

2   Electrical goods

3   Furniture

4   Damage to private property

5   Cars

6   Audio/computer

7   Professional services

8   Building

9   Dry-cleaners

10 Clothing

Source: Central Statistics Office Ireland

10
DEFUNCT HOLIDAYS

	Day	Holiday
1	19 March	St Joseph's Day
2	1 May	Sts Philip and James's Day
3	29 May	Birthday of Charles II
4	24 June	St John the Baptist's Day
5	29 June	Sts Peter and Paul's Day
6	1 August	Lammas Day
7	29 September	St Michael the Archangel's Day
8	21 October	Trafalgar Day
9	11 November	St Martin's Day, day of hiring fairs
10	14 November	Birthday of William III

After the institution of the Feast of the Immaculate Conception in 1708 by Pope Clement XI, there were 35 recognized Church holidays, as well as the movable feasts of Easter Monday and Tuesday, Ascension Thursday, Whit Monday and Tuesday and Corpus Christi. In 1800 Good Friday was made a public holiday. In colonial times the sovereign's birthday was also regarded as a holiday. During Queen Victoria's reign (1837–1901) her birthday (24 May) and the dates of her accession, marriage and coronation were all public half-holidays. On the instigation of Clare MP Colman O'Loghlen and Englishman John Lubbock, four bank holidays were created in 1871 – Easter and Whit Monday, the first Monday in August and St Stephen's Day. St Patrick's Day became a bank holiday in 1903. In Northern Ireland the date of the Whit Monday bank holiday was changed to the last Monday in May in 1971 and the August bank holiday was changed to the end of the month in 1972. 1 May became a bank holiday as May Day in Northern Ireland in 1971 and as Labour Day in the Republic in 1994. In 1916, 22 April was declared a bank holiday.

FASTEST-GROWING
RELIGIOUS AFFILIATIONS
in the Republic of Ireland

	Religion	Percentage increase*
1	Apostolic	157.5
2	Orthodox	99.3
3	Hindu	96.3
4	Atheist	85.8
5	Lutheran	72.1
6	Muslim	69.9
7	Buddhist	67.3
8	Brethren	64.4
9	Pantheist	52.9
10	Mormon	48.5

* Between 2001 and 2006 Censuses
Source: Central Statistics Office Ireland

TOP 10

LARGEST RELIGIOUS AFFILIATIONS

	Religion	Percentage of population	Members*
1	Catholic	69.89	4,141,068
2	Church of Ireland	6.30	373,399
3	Presbyterian	6.23	369,324
4	Christian other	2.09	123,624
5	Methodist	1.17	69,206
6	Muslim	0.40	23,575
7	Orthodox	0.18	10,437
8=	Buddhist	0.06	3,894
=	Evangelical	0.06	3,780
=	Hindu	0.06	3,699

* Figures for 2001
Source: Central Statistics Office Ireland and Northern Ireland Census Office

TOP 10

LARGEST RELIGIOUS AFFILIATIONS
in the Republic of Ireland

	Religion	Members*
1	Catholic	3,644,965
2	No religion	175,252
3	Church of Ireland (including Protestant)	118,948
4	Not stated	66,750
5	Other stated religions	54,033
6	Muslim (Islamic)	31,779
7	Other Christian religions	28,028
8	Presbyterian	21,496
9	Orthodox	19,994
10	Methodist	10,768

* Figures for 2009
Source: Central Statistics Office Ireland

TOP10

SMALLEST RELIGIOUS AFFILIATIONS
in the Republic of Ireland

	Religion	Members*
1	Brethren	365
2	Baha'i	504
3	Quaker	882
4	Atheist	929
5	Mormon	1,237
6	Agnostic	1,515
7	Pantheist	1,691
8	Jewish	1,930
9	Baptist	3,338
10	Jehovah's Witness	5,152

* Figures for 2006
Source: Central Statistics Office Ireland

TOP 10
BIGGEST LOTTERY WINS

	Date	Winner(s)	Lottery	Winnings (€)
1	29 Jul 2005	Dolores McNamara (Limerick)	EuroMillions	115,436,126
2	12 Jun 2009	Family group	EuroMillions	29,430,608
3	28 Jun 2008	Dan Morrissey Syndicate (Carlow)	Lotto	18,963,441
4	14 Apr 2010	Family group (Dungarvan)	Lotto	16,717,717
5	28 Jul 2007	Cunningham family (Cork City)	Lotto	16,185,749
6	26 Apr 2008	Family (Clondalkin)	Lotto	15,658,143
7	4 Jul 2008	Family group	EuroMillions	15,000,000
8	12 Mar 2008	Group of two (Co. Kildare)	Lotto	14,543,033
9	18 Apr 2009	Couple (Glenageary)	Lotto	14,530,193
10	22 Dec 2007	Family (Co. Galway)	Lotto	13,295,379

The largest unclaimed Lotto jackpot is an English Lotto ticket sold in Belfast on 14 July 2004. It was worth £20 million.

10 THINGS JUST AS LIKELY TO HAPPEN AS WINNING THE LOTTO JACKPOT

1   Meeting your long-lost brother randomly in New York

2   Having sextuplets or having two sets of twins

3   Being injured in an escalator accident

4   Catching amyloidosis, a rare liver disease

5   Dying in an aeroplane crash

6   Catching lupus

7   Being attacked by a shark

8   Your child having Progeria Syndrome (accelerated ageing disease)

9   Your dog or cat contracting the rabies virus *after* it has been
    vaccinated

10 Being struck by lightning (estimated odds vary from 7–10
    million/1)

> The odds of picking six numbers out of 45 to win the Lotto jackpot are 8,145,060/1.
> This is up from 1,947,792/1 when it started in 1986; 3,262,623/1 between 1992 and
> 1994; and 5,245,786/1 between 1994 and 2006. On average your six numbers would
> come up once every 270 years.

TOP 10
MOST POPULAR LEAVING CERT SUBJECTS

	Subject	Number of students*
1	Mathematics	101,872
2	English	101,850
3	Irish	92,989
4	Religious education	86,849
5	Physical education	63,762
6	French	59,970
7	Biology	55,011
8	Geography	48,706
9	Business studies	36,141
10	Home economics	26,553

* Figures for 2008
Source: Department of Education and Science

THE 10

LEAST POPULAR LEAVING CERT SUBJECTS

	Subject	Number of students*
1	Economic history	0
2	Greek	13
3	Agricultural economics	84
4	Orchestra	94
5	Keyboarding	196
6	Typewriting	232
7	Latin	264
8	Italian	465
9	Speech and drama	585
10	Classical studies	1,124

* Figures for 2008
Source: Department of Education and Science

LEAVING CERT SUBJECTS WITH THE HIGHEST PROPORTION OF HONOURS CANDIDATES

	Subject	Percentage*
1	English	61
2=	Biology	35
=	Geography	35
4=	French	27
=	Irish	27
6	Business studies	23
7	Home economics	17
8	Mathematics	16
9=	Art	15
=	History	15

* Figures for 2008
Source: Department of Education and Science

LEAVING CERT SUBJECTS WITH THE HIGHEST PROPORTION OF A GRADES

	Subject	Percentage*
1	Applied mathematics	27
2	Physics and chemistry	26
3	Chemistry	24
4=	Accounting	20
=	Physics	20
6	Biology	17
7	Spanish	16
8=	German	15
=	Music	15
10	Mathematics	14

* Figures for 2008
Source: Department of Education and Science

MOST DANGEROUS ROADS

Road	Casualties per km (0.62 mile)*
1 **N14 from NI border to N13, Co. Donegal** Distance: 20 km (12½ miles); 71 dead or seriously injured	3.58
2 **A29 from Moneymore Road to Kingsbridge, Co. Tyrone** Distance: 4 km (2½ miles); 13 dead or seriously injured	3.25
3 **N30 from Enniscorthy to Jamestown, Co. Wexford** Distance: 4.15 km (2½ miles); 11 dead or seriously injured	2.65
4 **N2 from Monaghan to NI border, Co. Monaghan** Distance: 16 km (10 miles); 41 dead or seriously injured	2.53
5 **N59 from Ballina to Dromore West, Co. Mayo** Distance: 25 km (15½ miles); 60 dead or seriously injured	2.4
6 **N53 from M1 to NI border, Co. Louth** Distance: 11 km (6¾ miles); 25 dead or seriously injured	2.34
7 **N5 from Longford to Cloonsgannagh, Co. Longford** Distance: 14 km (8¾ miles); 31 dead or seriously injured	2.24
8 **A3 from Moira to Lisburn, Co. Antrim** Distance: 11 km (6¾ miles); 22 dead or seriously injured	2
9 **A50 from Portadown to Banbridge, Co. Armagh** Distance: 13 km (8 miles); 22 dead or seriously injured	1.69
10 **N81 from Closh Cross to Tullow, Co. Carlow** Distance: 9 km (5½ miles); 15 dead or seriously injured	1.68

* Figures for 2002–06

THE 10
WORST YEARS FOR DEATHS ON THE ROADS*

	Year	Deaths
1	1972	640
2	1978	628
3	1979	614
4	1974	594
5	1973	592
6	1975	586
7	1977	583
8	1971	576
9	1981	572
10	1980	564

* Figures for the Republic of Ireland
Sources: National Roads Authority/ERU/Fíorais Thimpistí/Bóthair/RSA

In 1972, 368 people were killed in Northern Ireland, making a record 1,008 casualties on the island as a whole. This is Ireland's worst ever year for road accidents to date.

HOLIDAY DESTINATIONS

	Destination	Number of visitors*
1	England	1.9 million
2	Spain	1.6 million
3	France	780,000
4	Portugal	450,000
5	USA	410,000
6	Wales	360,000
7	Italy	240,000
8	Scotland	156,000
9	Germany	142,196
10	Greece	135,000

* Figures for 2008
Source: Various tourist boards

TOP 10
SUN RESORTS VISITED*

1   Santa Ponsa, Majorca

2   Puerto del Carmen, Lanzarote

3   Playa del Ingles, Gran Canaria

4   Praia da Rocha, Algarve

5   Torremolinos, Spain

6   Salou, Spain

7   Kusadasi, Turkey

8   Bodrum, Turkey

9   Alcudia, Majorca

10 Hersonissos, Crete

* In 2008
Source: Irish Tour Operators Federation

IRELAND:
A VISITOR'S GUIDE

TOP 10

MOST POPULAR VISITOR ATTRACTIONS

	Attraction	Location	Number of visitors*
1	Guinness Storehouse	Dublin	1,038,910
2	Dublin Zoo	Dublin	932,000
3	Cliffs of Moher Centre	Co. Clare	808,310
4	Giant's Causeway Centre	Co. Antrim	751,693
5	National Gallery	Dublin	742,332
6	National Aquatic Centre	Co. Dublin	706,739
7	Book of Kells Exhibition	Dublin	541,364
8	Irish Museum of Modern Art (IMMA)	Dublin	440,000
9	National Museum of Ireland – Archaeology	Dublin	380,547
10	Dublin Castle	Dublin	365,000

* Figures for 2008
Source: Fáilte Ireland/Northern Ireland Tourist Board

MOST SUCCESSFUL TIDY TOWNS

	Town	Years won
1	Glenties, Co. Donegal	1958, 1959, 1960, 1962, 1995
2=	Ardagh, Co. Longford	1989, 1996, 1998
=	Rathvilly, Co. Carlow	1961, 1963, 1968
=	Trim, Co. Meath	1972, 1974, 1984
=	Westport, Co. Mayo	2001, 2006, 2008
6=	Ballyjamesduff, Co. Cavan	1966, 1967
=	Keadue, Co. Roscommon	1993, 2003
=	Kilsheelan, Co. Tipperary	1975, 1979
=	Malin, Co. Donegal	1970, 1991
=	Terryglass, Co. Tipperary	1983, 1997
=	Virginia, Co. Cavan	1964, 1965

Tidy Towns is an annual competition in the Republic of Ireland. It was established in 1958 and is Ireland's best-known local environmental initiative. Over 700 towns compete annually.

10 FAMOUS GARDENS

	Garden	Location
1	Altamount	Co. Carlow
2	Belvedere	Co. Westmeath
3	Birr Castle	Co. Offaly
4	Crom	Co. Fermanagh
5	Garnish Island	Co. Cork
6	Japanese Gardens	Co. Kildare
7	Killruddery	Co. Wicklow
8	Lisselan	Co. Cork
9	Mount Usher	Co. Wicklow
10	Powerscourt	Co. Wicklow

Belvedere has a Victorian walled garden and rolling parkland with numerous follies.

Killruddery contains the oldest formal gardens in Ireland. Walks dating to the seventeenth-century are flanked by hornbeam, lime and beech hedges that meet at two central points.

FAMOUS HOUSES

	House	Location
1	Avondale	Co. Wicklow
2	Carton	Co. Kildare
3	Castlerea	Co. Roscommon
4	Castletown	Co. Kildare
5	Farmleigh	Co. Dublin
6	Kylemore Abbey	Co. Galway
7	Mount Stewart	Co. Down
8	Muckross House	Co. Kerry
9	Russborough	Co. Wicklow
10	Strokestown	Co. Roscommon

Farmleigh, built in 1881, was the home of the Guinness brewing family. It is now the official Irish State Guest House.

The cut-stone, Tudor-revival mansion Muckross House, built 1839–43, is in the heart of the Killarney National Park.

10 FAMOUS CASTLES

	Castle	Location
1	Blarney	Co. Cork
2	Bunratty	Co. Clare
3	Cahir	Co. Tipperary
4	Carrickfergus	Co. Antrim
5	Donegal	Co. Donegal
6	Dublin	Dublin
7	Kilkenny	Co. Kilkenny
8	King John's	Co. Limerick
9	Lismore	Co. Waterford
10	Trim	Co. Meath

Cahir Castle, built in 1142, is one of Ireland's largest and best-preserved castles. The 1981 movie *Excalibur* was filmed here.

Once the largest castle in Ireland, Trim Castle, dating back to 1176, was home to Henry V of England. It was built over a period of 20 years and is the largest Anglo-Norman castle in Ireland.

MOST VISITED MUSEUMS
AND GALLERIES

	Museum/gallery	Location	Number of visitors*
1	National Gallery	Dublin	742,332
2	Book of Kells Exhibition	Dublin	541,364
3	Irish Museum of Modern Art (IMMA)	Dublin	440,000
4	National Museum of Ireland – Archaeology	Dublin	380,547
5	Kilmainham Gaol	Dublin	300,828
6	National Museum of Ireland – Decorative Arts and History	Dublin	300,418
7	W5	Belfast	282,756
8	Chester Beatty Library	Dublin	225,543
9	Hugh Lane Gallery	Dublin	203,207
10	Ulster Folk & Transport Museum	Cultra	190,580

* Figures for 2008
Source: Fáilte Ireland and Northern Ireland Tourist Board

TOP 10

MOST VISITED CASTLES AND COUNTRY HOUSES

	Castle/country house	Location	Number of visitors*
1	Dublin Castle	Dublin	365,000
2	Blarney Castle	Co. Cork	360,000
3	Bunratty Castle	Co. Clare	305,557
4	Holy Cross Abbey	Co. Tipperary	260,000
5	Kilkenny Castle	Co. Kilkenny	256,533
6	Rock of Cashel	Co. Tipperary	237,732
7	Derry Walls	Derry	215,015
8	Farmleigh	Dublin	196,449
9	Kylemore Abbey	Co. Galway	180,000
10	Belvedere House	Co. Westmeath	164,211

* Figures for 2008
Source: Fáilte Ireland and Northern Ireland Tourist Board

PLACES ON JAMES JOYCE'S MAP
OF DUBLIN IN *ULYSSES*

	Place	Episode
1	Martello Tower, Sandycove	1 Telemachus
2	Clifton School, Dalkey	2 Nestor
3	Sandymount Strand	3 Proteus
4	Glasnevin Cemetery	6 Hades
5	Princes Street	7 Aeolus
6	National Library of Ireland	9 Scylla and Charybdis
7	Grafton Street	10 The Wandering Rocks
8	Ormond Hotel	11 Sirens
9	Barney Kiernans, now the Claddagh Ring, Little Britain Street	12 The Cyclops
10	Sandymount	13 Nausicaa

Joyce fans say that you could draw a map of Dublin in 1904 from the James Joyce map, *Ulysses*. It might not be altogether true, but it is a handy way to find a drink if you get transported back in time.

James Augustine Aloysius Joyce (1882–1941) was born at 41 Brighton Square, Rathgar, Dublin. He was educated at Clongowes, Belvedere and University College Dublin, and he pioneered the emerging stream-of-consciousness movement with *A Portrait of the Artist as a Young Man*, published in 1916, and *Ulysses*, published in 1922. Joyce settled in Paris in 1920 and began work on *Finnegan's Wake*, which was published in 1939. He died in Zurich, to where he had moved at the outbreak of the Second World War.

TOP 10

COUNTIES THAT ATTRACT THE HIGHEST NUMBER OF OVERSEAS VISITORS

	County	Number of visitors*
1	Dublin	8,320,000
2	Clare	685,000
3	Cork	609,000
4	Limerick	529,000
5	Galway	387,000
6	Waterford	356,000
7	Kilkenny	285,000
8	Wicklow	254,000
9	Wexford	243,000
10	Kerry	235,000

* Figures for 2007 in the Republic of Ireland
Source: Fáilte Ireland

VIEWS OF THE IRISH

1 ## Brendan Behan
'It's not that the Irish are cynical. It's rather that they have a wonderful lack of respect for everything and everybody.'

2 ## G. K. Chesterton
'Irish history is for England to remember and Ireland to forget.'

3 ## Winston Churchill
'We have always found the Irish a bit odd. They refuse to be English.'

4 ## James Joyce
'If Ireland is to become a new Ireland she must first become European.'

5 ## Hugh Leonard
'The problem with Ireland is that it's a country full of genius, but with absolutely no talent.'

6 ## Jack Nicholson
'I'm Irish. I think about death all the time.'

7 ## Flann O'Brien
'The majority of the members of the Irish Parliament are professional politicians, in the sense that otherwise they would not be given jobs minding mice at crossroads.'

8 ## Pope John Paul II
'Love is never defeated, and I could add, the history of Ireland proves it.'

9 ## J. M. Synge
'There is no language like the Irish for soothing and quieting.'

10 ## William Howard Taft
'If humour be the safety of our race, then it is due largely to the infusion into the American people of the Irish brain.'

10
OF THE OLDEST PUBS

1   ## The Brazen Head, Dublin
This site, outside the city walls and near the original bridge of Dublin, is said to have been a tavern since 1178. The deeds date to 1677 and the premises to 1781.

2   ## The Cock, Gormanstown, Co. Meath
It is claimed that this pub dates from 1390 and has been run by 21 generations of McCabes.

3   ## T & H Doolans, Waterford
The oldest tavern in Waterford, this establishment is said to date to 1400.

4   ## McHugh's, Belfast
This is the oldest pub and oldest building in Belfast. It dates to 1711.

5   ## Morahans, Ballinagare, Co. Roscommon
The Morahans have been running this pub since 1641. It is the longest that an establishment has been run by the same family.

6   ## Old Thatch, Killeagh, Co. Cork
The Old Thatch is the oldest thatched pub in Ireland and has been in the same family since 1667.

7   ## Grace O'Neill's, Donaghadee, Co. Down
This pub has the oldest title deeds, dating to 1611.

8   ## Sean's Bar, Athlone, Co. Westmeath
On the site of a wattle alehouse, it is thought that it dates back to 900. This is believed to be the oldest pub in Ireland.

9   White Lady, Kinsale, Co. Cork
This site is said to date to 1400.

10   White's Tavern, Belfast
The oldest pub in Belfast, the deeds date to 1630.

Bushmill's Distillery, Co. Antrim, was licensed in 1608 and is the oldest distillery in Ireland. St Francis Abbey, Kilkenny, is the oldest brewery, operating since the 14th century. Peter Smithwick began brewing there in 1710. Hilden, Co. Antrim, is Ireland's oldest microbrewery and was founded in 1981.

In 1610 Barnaby Rich declared, 'It is as rare a thing to find a house in Dublin without a tavern as it is to find a tavern without a strumpet.' When the first proper records of public houses were compiled as a result of the Licensing Act of 1635, there were 1,180 pubs in Dublin catering for 4,000 families.

10 PLACES AND THE SONGS THEY INSPIRED

Place and song title	Composer, lyricist or artist
1 'Aghadoe'	John Todhunter
2 'Avondale'	Dominic Behan
3 'Belfast'	Boney M
4 'Galway Bay'	Bing Crosby
5 'Killarney'	M. W. Balfe
6 'Lisdoonvarna'	Christy Moore
7 'Lough Ree'	Patrick Farrell
8 'Mountains of Mourne'	Percy French
9 'Skibbereen'	Trad/Sinead O'Connor
10 'Spancil Hill'	Michael Considine

BUSIEST AIRPORTS

	Airport	Number of passengers*
1	Dublin	23,500,000
2	Belfast International	5,262,354
3	Cork	3,250,000
4	Shannon	3,100,000
5	Belfast City	2,570,742
6	Knock	630,170
7	Derry	439,033
8	Kerry	420,000
9	Galway	270,000
10	Waterford	144,000

* Figures for 2008
Source: Individual airport authorities

TOP 10

DESTINATIONS OUT OF DUBLIN AIRPORT

1   London (5 airports)

2   Paris (2 airports)

3   Cork

4   Manchester (2 airports)

5   Birmingham

6   Frankfurt (2 airports)

7   Amsterdam

8   Edinburgh

9   Shannon

10 Nottingham East Midlands

Source: Dublin Airport Authority

UNIQUELY IRISH

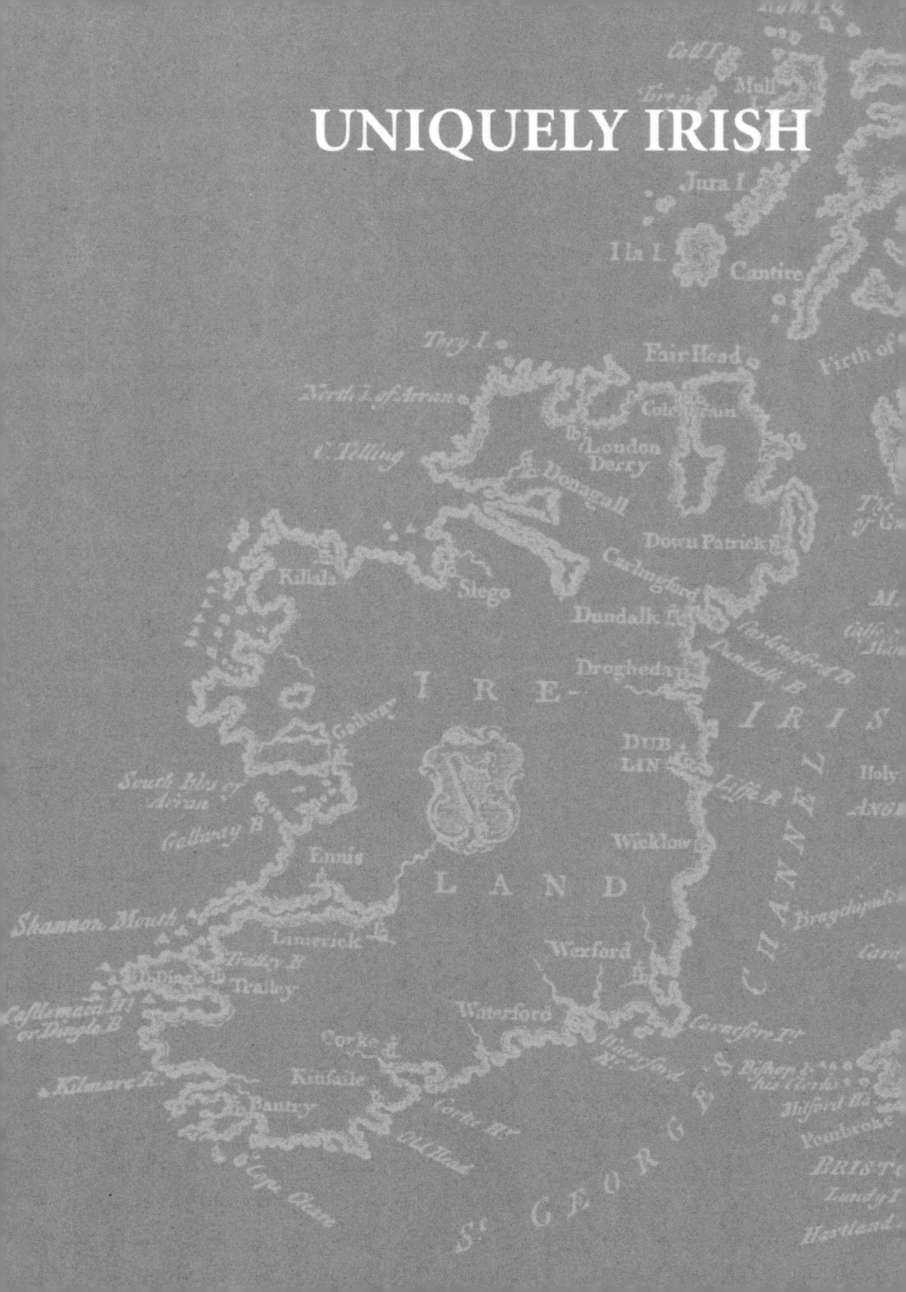

10
UNITS OF MEASUREMENT

1   Dublin Mean Time
    Until 1916, Dublin Mean Time was 25 mins behind Greenwich Mean Time. Prior to 1880, when Dublin Mean Time was extended to the whole of Ireland, Belfast was 1 min 19 secs ahead of Dublin, Cork was 11 mins behind.

2   Irish mile
    An Irish mile was equivalent to 2.048 km (6,720 ft). An English mile is 1.609 km (5,279 ft). For example, 11 Irish miles were equal to approximately 14 English miles.

3   Irish acre
    This traditional unit of land measurement was equivalent to 0.655 ha (just over 1½ English statute acres). For example, 30¼ Irish acres were equal to 49 English acres. This measurement was also sometimes called the Irish plantation acre.

4   Irish perch (also called an Erse pole)
    This unit of length measurement was equivalent to 6.4 m (7 yd). An English perch was 5 m (5½ yd).

5   Cunningham acre
    This was a measurement used in Ulster in Plantation times; it was equivalent to 0.52 ha (1¼ statute acres).

6   Cunningham perch
    The Cunningham perch was slightly shorter than the Irish perch, being 5.7 m (6¼ yd).

7   Celtic calendar
    The calendar began with the dark half of the year, Samain, usually 1 November (11 November in Gaelic Scotland), followed by Imbolc on 1 or 2 February. The light half of the year began on Bealtaine, 1 May (15 May in Scotland), followed by Lughnasa on 1 August (in Scotland sometimes as late as 29 September).

8   **Celtic months**
    Celtic months lasted 29 or 30 days and were divided into halves. An extra month of 30 days
    was added every third year to correspond with the solar calendar.

9   **Celtic Easter**
    Celtic Easter could be three weeks later than Roman Easter, as it was calculated using a table
    associated with St Jerome. Celtic Easter was retained on remote western islands such as
    the Skelligs until the 1800s, offering hasty couples the opportunity to get married there
    during Lent.

10 **Irish year**
    For 170 years Ireland had two calendars. The Gregorian calendar was adopted by the
    Catholics in 1582, but not by the English until 1752. The gap between the old-style (Julian)
    and new-style (Gregorian) calendars was ten days up to 28 February 1700 (old style), and
    11 days thereafter. While the Irish and Spanish celebrated Christmas just before the Battle
    of Kinsale in 1601, the English had yet to do so.

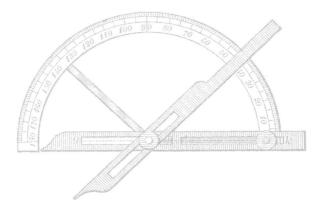

10
FAMOUS MEMBERS OF THE TRAVELLING COMMUNITY

1   Francie Barrett (b. Galway; 1977–)
    Francie Barrett is a light middleweight boxer who was the youngest member of the Irish
    team at the 1996 Atlanta Olympics.

2   Margaret Barry (b. Cork; 1917–89)
    A traditional singer and banjo player.

3   Johnny Doran (b. Rathnew, Co. Wicklow; 1909–50)
    An influential piper.

4   Pádraig 'Pecker' Dunne (b. Castlebar, Co. Mayo; 1932–)
    Traditional banjo player who has performed in England, France, Australia and New York.

5   Finbar Furey (b. Dublin; 1948–)
    Finbar was the best known of the Furey brothers, a traditional group with four brothers
    and Davey Arthur whose signature hit, 'The Green Fields of France', was in the Irish singles
    chart for 28 weeks. He contributed a song for Martin Scorsese's *Gangs of New York* in which
    he has a small role.

6   Michael Gomez (b. Longford; 1977–)
    Born Michael Armstrong, he held the WBU super-featherweight title in 2004–5.

7   Nan Joyce (1940–)
    Joyce was the first Traveller to stand in a national election, in 1982, and author of *My Life on
    the Road*, published in 1985.

8   Winnie Maughan (1994–)
    She is the actress-star of the breakthrough film about the Travelling community, *Pavee
    Lackeen (The Traveller Girl)*, released in 2005.

9   Nora 'Oney' Power (1861–1937)
    Power was a folklorist who worked with Pádraig Mac Gréine in collecting tales from the
    Travelling community.

10 John Reilly (b. probably Carrick-on-Shannon, Co. Leitrim;
    1926–69)

    A traditional singer who was a major influence on Christy Moore.

RIDDLES FROM THE SONG TRADITION

1 **'Bantry Girls Lament'**
Johnny going to fight 'the King of Spain' would have been unlikely at the time of composition; Johnny would have been more likely to have fought on behalf of the King of Spain.

2 **'Boolavogue'**
If the sun is setting over the 'bright May meadows of Shelmalier' it is setting in the east.

3 **'Boston Burglar'**
Bound for Charlestown? There is no jail in Charlestown.

4 **'Carrickfergus'**
Ballycran, or indeed the nonexistent Ballygrand, are nowhere near Carrickfergus, nor is Kilkenny, which is referred to in the second verse.

5 **'Holy Ground'**
The song, played when Pope John Paul II arrived in Ireland in 1979, is ironic: it refers to the red-light district in Cobh, Co. Cork.

6 **'Merry Ploughboy'**
Though the song refers to 'Easter Week', the Thompson Gun wasn't invented until 1919 and not used until the last month of the War of Independence.

7 **'Spancil Hill' (1)**
The 23rd of June is the day of the fair in Spancil Hill, not the day before the fair.

8 **'Spancil Hill' (2)**
Author Michael Considine's sweetheart was 'Mac, the ranger's daughter' and not 'Ned, the farmer's daughter'.

9 **'Spanish Lady'**
The same 'Spanish Lady' has featured in two different Dublin versions, several in London, and one in Chester, Galway City and Belfast.

10 **'Whiskey in the Jar'**
The Cork and Kerry mountains are two days' ride from where the highwayman of the song plied his trade.

FAIRY TREES

1   **Ardbraccan, Co. Meath**
This is said to have been the site of the Tree of Tortu (Bile Tartain), a giant ash tree that was regarded as the most sacred tree of ancient Ireland.

2   **Ballymagroarty, Co. Derry**
A road was rerouted in 1968 to protect a hawthorn bush.

3   **Dunmanogoe, Co. Kildare**
The sacred tree, the Yew of Mugna, is thought to have grown here.

4   **Farbill, Co. Westmeath**
Believed to have been the site of Daithi's Branch (Craeb Daithi), a sacred tree.

5   **Latoon, Newmarket, Co. Clare**
The N18 was rerouted in 1999 after a whitethorn was threatened with destruction.

6   **Lismullin, Co. Meath**
Work on the M3 motorway was halted in May 2007 after an ancient ceremonial enclosure was discovered.

7   **Old Leighlin, Co. Carlow**
This small town was said to be the site of the Yew of Ross, an ancient sacred tree.

8   **Rossnowlagh, Co. Donegal**
The county council stopped work on a road in 1969 because of a fairy bush.

9 Sooey, Co. Sligo

In December 2006, two new electricity poles were erected within a short distance of the fairy fort. Within a short time the poles were bent. The poles had to be re-erected twice more. Strong winds were blamed, but locals believed that the powers of the fairy fort played their part.

10 Uisneach, Co. Westmeath

This was the site of the Celtic Festival of Bealtaine and the Tree of Uisneach (Bile Uisneg).

10
PISEOGS

1   If someone places a rotten egg in your garden it will bring you bad luck.

2   It is unlucky to break a glass on your wedding day.

3   If crows vacate your tree or crickets leave the house, someone in the family will die.

4   A white horse is an unlucky thing to see.

5   If a farmer harms a swallow, blood will appear in the milk of his cows.

6   If a woman in childbirth wears her husband's waistcoat, it transfers some of the birth pangs to him.

7   If a pregnant woman steps over a grave the child will be born with a twisted foot.

8   Green is an unlucky colour to be worn on a wedding day.

9   Some women can cause misfortune by fixing their evil eye on you.

10 Some men can make any woman fall in love with them by drying their hands on her apron.

Piseog is an Irish word meaning superstition.

PATRON SAINTS

1   **St Brendan**
    Patronage: Travellers and explorers

2   **St Brigid**
    Patronage: Poets, dairy workers, blacksmiths, healers, cattle, fugitives, Irish nuns, midwives, newborn babies and scholars

3   **St Cathal**
    Patronage: Hernia sufferers

4   **St Columba**
    Patronage: Bookbinders, poets, Ireland, Scotland and against floods.

5   **St Dunchad**
    Patronage: Sailors

6   **St Dympna**
    Patronage: Mental illness, epilepsy, sleepwalkers and those possessed by the Devil

7   **St Fiacra**
    Patronage: Gardeners, horticulturists, venereal disease, haemorrhoids, and taxi drivers

8   **St Gall**
    Patronage: Birds

9   **St Oliver Plunkett**
    Patronage: Peace and reconciliation

10 **St Patrick**
    Patronage: Ireland and Nigeria

BETS PLACED WITH PADDY POWER

1   Xabi Alonso to score a goal from inside his own half – 125/1
He did, in 2006. One punter won £31,500 for his stake of £200.

2   Baracouda would not win at Cheltenham – Paul Ryan offered to run naked through Tallaght
The horse won. Ryan ran naked.

3   Eamon Dunphy to manage Sunderland – 1,000/1
He didn't.

4   Eamon Gilmore to become Labour leader – 11/1
He did.

5   Barack Obama to become next US president in May 2008 – 50/1
He did.

6   Joseph Ratzinger to become next Pope – 12/1
He did. (Francis Arinze from Nigeria leads the betting to be the next Pope at 5/1, with Father Dougal Maguire at 1,000/1.)

7   Seven-races accumulator – 42,000/1
A €10 bet won a record €424,710 for Catherine Egan from Roscommon in 2004.

8   Maggie Simpson shot Mr Burns – 500/1
She did.

9   U2 to represent Ireland in the Eurovision Song Contest – 500/1
They didn't.

10   White Christmas in 2004 – 5/1
Snow fell on 25 December 2004 and cost the bookies €50,000.

ICONIC IRISH PUBS OUTSIDE IRELAND

Pub name	Location
1 Beckett's	Budapest, Hungary
2 Irish Village	Dubai, UAE
3 Kitty O'Shea's	Brussels, Belgium
4 McSorley's	New York City, USA
5 Mercantile	Sydney, Australia
6 O'Neill's	Islington, London, England
7 Plough and the Stars	San Francisco, USA
8 Rosie McGee's	Copenhagen, Denmark
9 Rosie O'Grady's	New York City, USA
10 Le Bistrot Irlandais	Paris, France

10

COUNTIES AND THE FOODS THEY ARE ASSOCIATED WITH

	County	Food
1	Carlow	Scallions
2	Cavan	Bacon
3	Cork	Milk
4	Donegal	Fish
5	Dublin	Langoustines
6	Galway	Oysters
7	Kerry	Butter
8	Monaghan	Mushrooms
9	Tipperary	Cheese
10	Wexford	Strawberries

QUINTESSENTIAL DISHES

1   Bacon cooked with cabbage, cross-cut carrots, garlic and peppercorns

2   Beef served with Guinness

3   Black pudding flavoured with country herbs

4   Chicken casserole garnished with chopped parsley

5   Grouse with chestnuts and mixed herbs, cooked slowly

6   Kerry pies

7   Lamb cutlets served with honey, fruit and herbs

8   Oysters served with bacon

9   Pheasant stuffed with black pudding

10 Salmon, smoked and cooked, with cream and herbs

The filling for a Kerry pie consists of shoulder of lamb baked with onions, carrots, parsley and thyme.

10 WAYS WITH A POTATO

1 **Boxty**
Grated potatoes with a cup of flour, a teaspoon of bread soda and butter.

2 **Champ**
Traditionally made with onions, young nettles, parlsey, leeks, herbs or chives can be substituted.

3 **Coddle**
A Dublin dish, potatoes with slices of ham or bacon, pork sausages and onions or parsley.

4 **Colcannon**
A potato and cabbage dish traditional at Hallowe'en, best done with floury potatoes like Kerr's Pink.

5 **Potato cake**
Mash the potato, add flour, softened butter and season. Use good floury potatoes such as Kerr's Pink or Golden Wonder in winter. Eggs, cheese and apples are added. Celebrity chef Theodora FitzGibbon uses chopped peel.

6 **Potato soup**
Made with onions, butter, half a cup of milk or cream, and 850 ml (1½ pints) of chicken or beef stock. Cheese, parsley, chives or streaky rasher can be added.

7 **Potato skins**
Fillings include cheese, garlic, spinach and yoghurt.

8 **Shepherd's Pie**
Usually a 2:3 proportion between the minced beef or lamb and potatoes, with added onions and carrots.

9 **Traditional mash**
Parsley, butter, milk, herbs, onions and Parmesan are popular additions.

10 **Traditional roast**
Choice of bacon fat or oil determines how crisp on the outside and how firm on the inside.

Over 70 ways of preparing potatoes are associated with Ireland, with favourite varieties including Rooster, Home Guard, British Queen, Golden Wonder, Kerr's Pink, Record, Pentland Dell and King Edward, according to season and dish. The original name (an Spáinneach) suggests they were introduced by the Spanish from South America.

THE CULTURAL ISLE

TOP 10
BESTSELLING FICTION BOOKS*

	Title	Author
1	*The Da Vinci Code*	Dan Brown
2	*Angels and Demons*	Dan Brown
3	*Harry Potter and the Deathly Hallows*	J. K. Rowling
4	*Harry Potter and the Half-blood Prince*	J. K. Rowling
5	*The Secret*	Rhonda Byrne
6	*Harry Potter and the Order of the Phoenix*	J. K. Rowling
7	*The Curious Incident of the Dog in the Night-time*	Mark Haddon
8	*New Moon*	Stephenie Meyer
9	*Digital Fortress*	Dan Brown
10	*The Secret Scripture*	Sebastian Barry

* Source: Based on life sales from the Nielsen Bestseller Charts, which took over
monitoring Irish bestsellers in 2002, up to October 2009

BESTSELLING AUTHORS

1   Cecelia Ahern (1981–)
    This Drumcondra-born, former-Taoiseach's daughter, made the charts with the 2004 best-
    seller *PS I Love You*.

2   Maeve Binchy (1940–)
    A former journalist, born in Dalkey, Binchy made her name with *Light a Penny Candle* in
    1982. Her signature novel, *Circle of Friends*, was made into a Hollywood movie in 1995.

3   John Boyne (1971–)
    Boyne's book, *The Boy in the Striped Pyjamas*, sold more than 5 million copies worldwide.

4   Eoin Colfer (1965–)
    His Artemis Fowl children's book series debuted in 2001.

5   John Connolly (1968–)
    This Dublin-born former journalist's *Every Dead Thing*, published in 1999, was a
    successful precursor to a crime series set in Maine.

6   Cathy Kelly (1963–)
    Born in Belfast and raised in Dublin, her debut success was *Woman to Woman* in 1997.

7   Marian Keyes (1963–)
    Born in Limerick, her 1995 debut, *Watermelon* was followed in 1996 by the signature *Lucy
    Sullivan is Getting Married*.

8   Frank McCourt (1930–2009)
    His controversial 1996 memoir *Angela's Ashes* won the Pulitzer Prize for Biography.

9   Joseph O'Connor (1963–)
    This Dún Laoghaire-born novelist's signature works are *Cowboys and Indians*, in 1991,
    which was shortlisted for the Whitbread Prize, and *Star of the Sea*, published in 2002.

10 Patricia Scanlan (1960–)
    This former librarian's debut success was *City Girls*, in 1990.

10 NOVELISTS

1   **Elizabeth Bowen (b. Dublin; 1899–1973)**
    Raised in Cork, Bowen wrote novels, short stories and non-fiction. She wrote her final novel, *Eva Trout,* in 1968.

2   **Oliver Goldsmith (b. Pallas, Co. Longford; 1728–74)**
    He published *The Vicar of Wakefield,* one of his best-known works, in 1766.

3   **Molly Keane (b. Newbridge, Co. Kildare; 1905–96)**
    Good Behaviour, written in 1981, was the first novel written under her own name. She had previously written under the pseudonym of M. J. Farrell.

4   **Charles Kickham (b. Mullinahone, Co. Tipperary; 1928–82)**
    He based his hugely successful novel *Knocknagow,* published in 1879, in his native town.

5   **John McGahern (b. Dublin; 1934–2006)**
    McGahern was raised in Aughawillan near Ballinamore, Co. Leitrim. His best-known work *Amongst Women,* was written in 1990.

6   **George Moore (b. Moore Hall, Co. Mayo; 1852–1933)**
    Among his many works, *A Drama in Muslin* (1886) and *Esther Waters* (1894) are two of the best known.

7   **Kate O'Brien (b. Limerick City; 1897–1974)**
    She won the James Tait Black Prize for *Without My Cloak,* written in 1931. Her other best-known works are *The Ante-Room* (1934), *The Land of Spices* (1941) and *That Lady* (1946).

8   **Brian O'Nolan** (b. Strabane, Co. Tyrone; 1911–66)
    His novels *At Swim-Two-Birds* (1939) and *The Third Policeman* (1940), both written under
    the pseudonym Flann O'Brien, achieved a cult following.

9   **Bram Stoker** (b. Clontarf; 1847–1912)
    His novel, *Dracula*, written in 1897, is the most successful horror novel of all time. The
    work was partly inspired by childhood attendance at funerals in the crypts of St Michan's
    Church in Dublin.

10 **Francis Stuart** (b. Australia; 1902–2000)
    Raised in Dublin, one of his best-known works is *Black List Section H*, written in 1971,
    which is regarded as an autobiographical novel.

10
20TH-CENTURY NOVELISTS*

1   John Banville (b. Enniscorthy; 1945–)
    The Sea, written in 2005, won the Booker Prize.

2   Sebastian Barry (b. Dublin; 1955–)
    A Long Long Way, written in 2005, was shortlisted for the Booker Prize.

3   Dermot Bolger (b. Finglas, Dublin; 1959–)
    His novel, *The Journey Home*, written in 1990, was a controversial bestseller in Ireland.

4   Roddy Doyle (b. Kilbarrack, Dublin; 1958–)
    Paddy Clarke Ha Ha Ha, written in 1993, won the Booker Prize. The Barrytown trilogy was adapted for the big screen: *The Commitments*, written in 1987, filmed in 1991; *The Snapper*, written in 1990, filmed in 1993; and *The Van*, written in 1991 and shortlisted for the Booker Prize in that same year, filmed in 1996.

5   Anne Enright (b. Rathmines; 1962–)
    The Gathering, written in 2007, won the Booker Prize.

6   Aidan Higgins (b. Celbridge; 1927–)
    His childhood was the inspiration for his first novel, *Langrishe, Go Down*, written in 1966.

7   Tom Kilroy (b. Callan, Co. Kilkenny; 1934–)
    The Big Chapel, written in 1971, was shortlisted for the Booker Prize.

8   Edna O'Brien (b. Tuamgraney, Co. Clare; 1930–)
    Her first novel, *The Country Girls*, was written in 1960.

9   Colm Tóibín (b. Enniscorthy, Co. Wexford; 1955–)
    His novel *The Master* was shortlisted for the 2004 Booker Prize and won the International IMPAC Dublin Literary Award in 2006.

10 William Trevor (b. Mitchelstown, Co. Cork; 1928–)
    He is a three-time Whitbread Prize winner for: *The Children of Dynmouth*, written in 1976; *Fools of Fortune*, 1983; and *Felicia's Journey*, 1994.

    * Entries give an example of a signature work(s)

PLAYWRIGHTS*

1   **Samuel Beckett (b. Dublin; 1906–89)**
    Waiting for Godot was written in 1952. Beckett was awarded the Nobel Prize in Literature in 1969.

2   **Brendan Behan (b. Dublin; 1923–64)**
    The Quare Fellow, written in 1954, was his first play.

3   **Brian Friel (b. Omagh, Co. Tyrone; 1929–)**
    Dancing at Lughnasa was written in 1990. It was made into a film in 1998. The screenplay was written by Frank McGuinness (see below) and starred Meryl Streep.

4   **John B. Keane (b. Listowel, Co. Kerry; 1928–2002)**
    The Field, written in 1965, was adapted for Jim Sheridan's 1990 film starring Richard Harris.

5   **Martin McDonagh (b. London to expatriate Irish parents; 1970–)**
    The Beauty Queen of Leenane, written in 1996, has won many awards, including four Tony awards for the Broadway production.

6   **Frank McGuinness (b. Buncrana, Co. Donegal; 1953–)**
    Observe the Sons of Ulster Marching Towards the Somme, written in 1985, won him the London Evening Standard Award for Most Promising Playwright.

7   **Tom Murphy (b. Tuam, Co. Galway; 1935–)**
    His play, *A Crucial Week in the Life of a Grocer's Assistant*, written in 1969, was first performed at the Abbey Theatre in Dublin.

8   **Sean O'Casey (b. Dublin; 1880–1964)**
    The Plough and the Stars (1926) provoked a riot when it was first performed at the Abbey Theatre in Dublin.

9   **George Bernard Shaw (b. Dublin; 1856–1950)**
    Heartbreak House (1919) was first performed at the Garrick Theatre in New York.

10 **Oscar Wilde (b. Dublin; 1854–1900)**
    The Importance of Being Earnest (1895) was first performed at the St James's Theatre in London. The play has been adapted for the big screen three times.

* Entries detail one example of each playwright's work

10
POETS

1   **William Allingham (1824–89)**
    This Ballyshannon poet brought generations of Irish children 'up the airy mountain and down the rushy glen'.

2   **Thomas Davis (1814–45)**
    Davis was born in Mallow, Co. Cork, and was a patriotic balladeer and author of a 'Nation Once Again'.

3   **Patrick Kavanagh (1904–67)**
    Anti-pastoral Inniskeen poet known for the epic 'The Great Hunger' (1942) and the signature 'Stony Grey Soil' (1947), while 'On Raglan Road' (1946) sung by Luke Kelly (1940–84), became an iconic ballad.

4   **Seamus Heaney (1939–)**
    From Bellaghy, Co. Derry, Heaney won the Nobel Prize in Literature in 1995. His early signature poem, 'Digging', has been overtaken by 'Requiem for the Croppies' in popular culture.

5   **John Hewitt (1907–87)**
    From Belfast, John Hewitt's poem 'The Colony' explored the planter's relationship with the landscape.

6   **Francis Ledwidge (1887–1917)**
    This war poet from Slane died at Ypres. He is best known for 'Thomas McDonagh' and 'The Blackbirds'.

7   **Michael Longley (1939–)**
    From Belfast, Longley's signature poems include 'The Greengrocer' (1979) and 'Gorse Fires' (1991).

8   Derek Mahon (1941–)
    This famously reticent Belfast poet's signature work is 'A Disused Shed in Co. Wexford',
    published in 1975.

9   Thomas Moore (1779–1852)
    From Dublin, Moore was the author of hundreds of patriotic and nostalgic songs set to
    Irish tunes. His most notable works are 'The Harp That Once Through Tara's Halls' and
    'The Minstrel Boy'.

10 W. B. Yeats (1865–1939)
    Yeats won the Nobel Prize in Literature in 1923. From over 1,000 published poems, 'Sailing
    to Byzantium', 'The Stolen Child', 'An Irish Airman Foresees His Death' and 'The Second
    Coming' have endured in popular culture.

10 TRAVEL WRITERS

1   St Brendan (b. nr Tralee, Co. Kerry; *c.* 484–577)
We can't be sure he wrote it, but *Navigatio Sancti Brendani* (*The Navigation of Saint Brendan*) was a medieval equivalent of an international bestseller and is one of the most influential travel books of all time.

2   Gerald Hanley (b. Liverpool to an Irish family; 1916–92)
Hanley wrote about his travels to post-colonial societies.

3   Seosamh Mac Grianna (b. Rannafast, Co. Donegal; 1900–90)
His classic travel books in the Irish language include *An Bhreatain Bheag*, written in 1933, and *Na Lochlannaigh*, written in 1938.

4   Dervla Murphy (b. Lismore, Co. Waterford; 1931–)
She launched her career in 1965 with the story of her bicycle journey from Ireland to India, entitled *Full Tilt: Ireland to India with a Bicycle*.

5   Robert Lloyd Praeger (b. Holywood, Co. Down; 1865–1953)
Praeger wrote about how his passion for botany brought him new experiences.

6   Michael Joseph Quin (b. Thurles, Co. Tipperary; 1796–1843)
His book *A Steam Voyage Down the Danube*, written in 1835, was a bestseller.

7   Walter Starkie (b. Killiney, Co. Dublin; 1894–1976)
Starkie was an authority on the Romany people, travelling with them and writing about his experiences. His works include *Raggle-Taggle: Adventures with a Fiddle in Hungary and Romania*, written in 1933.

8   Laurence Sterne (b. Clonmel, Co. Tipperary; 1713–68)
His influential *A Sentimental Journey through France and Italy*, written in 1768 following a journey to France in 1762, opined that feelings are more interesting than landscapes.

9   J. M. Synge (b. Rathfarnham, Dublin; 1871–1909)
Synge spent six summers living on the Aran Islands. He celebrated his experience of Irish country people in four books.

10   Isaac Weld (b. Dublin; 1774–1856)
His 1807 title *Scenery of Killarney* was a record of his time spent sailing the lakes of Killarney in a boat made from compressed brown paper.

JOURNALISTS

1 **Peter Finnerty** (b. Loughrea, Co. Galway; c.1766–1822)
Founded *The Press* newspaper in Dublin in 1797. He was the first accredited war correspondent, and covered the Napoleonic wars in 1809.

2 **Frank Gallagher** (b. Cork; 1893–1962)
First editor of the *Irish Press*.

3 **John Gray** (b. Claremorris, Co. Mayo; 1815–75)
Gray transformed the *Freeman's Journal* from a small-circulation newsletter into a mass-market newspaper; a specialist sports section was among his innovations.

4 **Alfred Harmsworth** (b. Palmerstown; 1865–1922)
His experience in Dublin with a cycling magazine inspired him to pioneer the English tabloid newspaper, starting first the *Daily Mail*, then the *Daily Mirror,* and he purchased London's *The Times* newspaper.

5 **Tom Kettle** (b. Dublin; 1880–1916)
He was a war correspondent for the *Daily News* before he was killed in action in Ginchy.

6 **Charles Lucas** (b. Ennistymon; 1713–71)
Lucas was a political agitator who founded the *Freeman's Journal*, the most influential newspaper of its era.

7 **P. D. Mehigan** (b. Cork; 1884–1965)
Mehigan pioneered a sports-writing style in the Irish idiom under the pen name Carbery.

8 **T. P. O'Connor** (b. Athlone; 1848–1929)
He identified the changing taste of industrial England, fulfilling the appetite for celebrity and sports news with the original *Star* newspaper in 1891.

9 **Sir William Howard Russell** (b. Tallaght; 1820–1907)
Russell established the concept and credibility of the war correspondent while covering the Crimean War.

10 **John Wyse Power** (b. Waterford; 1864–1926)
Power was a founding member of the Gaelic Athletic Association (GAA) and first editor of the *Evening Herald*.

10
WONDERS OF MEDIEVAL IRELAND ACCORDING TO GERALD OF WALES

1   'Lakes in North Munster...
     ...with two islands, on one of which any woman or animal or bird of the female sex that
     enters will die immediately, while no one has ever died or could die a natural death on the
     smaller island, an island lake in Ulster visited by angels and saints on one side inhabited by
     evil spirits on the other side, ready to seize anyone willing to attempt to spend a night in
     one of the nine pits there.' (Lakes identified as Loch Cre, now dried up near Roscrea, and
     Lough Derg in Co. Donegal.)

2   'An island...
     ...where human corpses exposed in the open do not putrefy, and where there is not a single
     mouse.' (Inis Gluaire, Erris, Co. Mayo.)

3   'Wells in Munster...
     ...where anyone who washes instantly turns grey, in Leinster where if a man washes in it he
     will not get greyer, on a mountain top in Connacht which ebbs and overflows three times a
     day and the enchanted well that was kept permanently covered in Ulster, until one day a
     woman left it uncovered and it overflowed and covered the surrounding neighbourhood.'
     (Slieve Bloom and the source of the Gallorn, Co. Monaghan, and Lough Neagh.)

4   'Pile of stones...
     ...brought by giants from Africa, transferred from a hill in Kildare to Britain.' (Stonehenge.)

5   'The man in Ossory...
     ...who changed into the form of a wolf for seven years, the woman in Limerick with a beard
     and the man in Wicklow who was half an ox and half a man.'

6   'How Kevin's willow tree...
     ...in Glendalough gives a white fruit, and Colman's ducks are tame and, when killed, cannot
     be cooked.'

7   'The stone in Munster...
     ...which each morning miraculously contains wine enough to say masses for the day.'

8   'The bell that returns...
    ...to Clonard unless it is exorcised every night, the fire that never goes out in Kildare and
    whose ashes never increase.'

9   'The cross in Dublin...
    ... that speaks.'

10 'Mills in Ossory...
    ...that will not grind corn on Sundays and in Fore that women cannot enter, the wheat
    cursed by the bishop of Cork that would not grow, the mill of St Luthernus.'

Giraldus (de Barry) Cambrensis (1146–1223) was a Pembrokeshire-born bishop and
cousin of the FitzGerald ancestors. He visited Ireland as secretary to Prince John in
1184. He wrote two books, *Topographia Hibernica* (*Topography of Ireland*) in 1187 and
Expugnatio Hibernica (*The Conquest of Ireland*) in 1188, in which he described the land
and people, often in hostile terms.

10 BANNED LITERARY WORKS

	Title	Author	First published
1	*Brave New World*	Aldous Huxley	1931
2	*Catch-22*	Joseph Heller	1961
3	*The Country Girls*	Edna O'Brien	1960
4	*The Dark*	John McGahern	1965
5	*Eyeless in Gaza*	Aldous Huxley	1936
6	*A Farewell to Arms*	Ernest Hemingway	1929
7	*The Grapes of Wrath*	John Steinback	1939
8	*Lady Chatterley's Lover*	D. H. Lawrence	1928
9	*The Tailor and Ansty*	Eric Cross	1942
10	*Ulysses*	James Joyce	From 1918 (in serial form)

WRITERS' PSEUDONYMS

Pseudonym	Real name
1 Æ	George Russell
2 Corno di Bassetto	George Bernard Shaw (when music critic of *The Star* in the 1880s)
3 M. J. Farrell	Molly Keane
4 Hugh Leonard	Jack Keyes Byrne
5 Flann O'Brien (also used Myles na gCopaleen)	Brian O'Nolan
6 Ross O'Carroll Kelly	Paul Howard
7 Frank O'Connor	Michael O'Donovan
8 M'Florr Ó'Squarr (among many others!)	Jonathan Swift
9 Speranza	Jane Francesca Wilde (mother of Oscar)
10 Zozimus	Michael Moran

George Russell's pseudonym was a misprint. He had intended it to be Æ'on, the name given by Gnostics to the earliest beings separated by God. However, he liked the misprint and kept it.

Molly Keane's pseudonym until 1981, M. J. Farrell, was borrowed from the name of a pub.

POETS IN THE IRISH LANGUAGE

1   Piaras Feiritéar (b. probably Kerry; 1600–53)
    This soldier-poet enlivened the formal Irish poetry of his age with French-style love
    poems.

2   Pádraigín Haicéad (b. probably nr Cashel, Co. Tipperary;
    c.1600–54)
    His stirring martial poetry of the 1640s made him the leading poet of his generation.

3   Michael Hartnett (b. Croom, Co. Limerick; 1941–99)
    His *Cúlú Íde*, written in 1975, celebrated a move from the confines of writing in English
    to the larger Irish vocabulary.

4   Brian Merriman (b. Ennistymon, Co. Clare; 1749–1805)
    His raunchy *Cúirt an Mheán Oíche*, written in 1780, is the most-read Irish language text.
    It scandalized church and civil authorities alike.

5   Dáibhí Ó Bruadair (b. Carrigtwohill, Co. Cork; 1625–98)
    He gave a valuable Irish perspective on the social upheavals of the 17th century.

6   Máirtín Ó Direáin (b. Inishmore, Aran Islands; 1910–88)
    His *Rogha Dánta*, written in 1949, contrasts his island upbringing with an urban
    environment.

7   Tadhg Ó Donnchadha (pseudonym 'Tórna') (b. Carrignavar, Co.
    Cork; 1874–1949)
    His dull but worthy *Leoithne Andeas*, written in 1905, was the first collection of poems in
    Irish of the literary revival.

8   Antoine Ó Raifteiri (b. Killeden, Co. Mayo; 1784–1835)
    This blind poet's work had an irreverent take on pre-Famine Ireland.

9   Aodhagán Ó Rathaille (b. Scrahanaveal, Co. Kerry; 1670–1729)
    He was a master of the dream-poem – the 'Aisling', and of infusing impassioned speech
    into the formal style of his time.

10 Seán Ó Ríordáin (b. Ballyvourney, Co. Cork; 1916–77)
    Ó Ríordáin infused European modernism into Irish poetry with *Eireaball Spideoige*
    in 1952.

WRITERS OF NOVELS AND MEMOIRS IN IRISH

1   Máirtín Ó Cadhain (b. Connemara; 1906–70)
    His signature novel, *Cré na Cille* (*Graveyard Soil*), is a conversation among arrivals in a
    graveyard that reads like a *Father Ted* script.

2   Pádraic Ó Conaire (b. Galway; 1882–1928)
    He is famous for his story of a dishonest salesman and his wife trying to get an exaggerated
    price for a lazy donkey, *M'asal Beag Dubh* (*My Little Black Donkey*).

3   Tomás Ó Criomhthain (b. Great Blasket Island; 1856–1937)
    His worthy but dull memoir *An tOileánach* (*The Islandman*), written in 1929, started the
    genre of Blasket Island biographies.

4   Liam Ó Flaithearta (b. Inishmore, Aran Islands; 1896–1984)
    Author of *Dúil* (*Desire*), published in 1953, a classic short-story collection.

5   Séamus Ó Grianna (b. Ranafast, Co. Donegal; 1889–1969) and
    Seosamh Mac Grianna (b. Ranafast, Co. Donegal; 1900–90)
    These two novelist brothers wrote in the Donegal dialect.

6   An tAthair Peadar Ó Laoghaire (b. Clondrohid, Co. Cork;
    1839–1920)
    He was author of literary folk tale *Séadna* in 1904.

7   Pádraig Ó Siochfhradha (b. Dingle, Co. Kerry; 1883–1964)
    Written using the pen name An Seabhac (The Hawk), his best-known novel written in
    1921, *Jimín Mháire Thaidhg*, is narrated by a child whose escapades go awry.

8   Muiris Ó Súilleabháin (b. Great Blasket Island; 1904–1950)
    His memoir *Fiche Bliain ag Fás* (*Twenty Years a'Growing*), written in 1933, mourns the
    passing of an island existence.

9   Eoghan Ó Tuairisc (b. Ballinasloe, Co. Galway; 1919–82)
    Ó Tuairisc wrote some of the first historical novels and thrillers in Irish, including
    L'Attaque, which was published in 1962.

10 Peig Sayers (b. Dingle, Co. Kerry; 1873–1958)
    This Dingle storyteller was badly served by the fact that her memoir, *Peig*, published in
    1936, emphasizing the humour in a bleak and often 'island' existence, was a compulsory
    text for a generation of schoolchildren.

10 COMPOSERS AND MUSICIANS

1   M. W. Balfe **(b. Dublin; 1808–70)**
    Balfe is best known for the opera *Bohemian Girl* (1843).

2   Phil Coulter **(b. Derry; 1942–)**
    He has a significant body of work. He co-wrote the Eurovision-winning song 'Puppet on a
    String' and the most successful Eurovision second-placed song 'Congratulations'. Coulter
    wrote 'Ireland's Call' for the Ireland rugby union team and one of his most popular songs is
    the haunting 'The Town I Loved So Well'.

3   Shaun Davey **(b. Belfast; 1948–)**
    Most well known as the composer of four large-scale concert works, including *The
    Brendan Voyage* and *Granuaile*. In 2003 he composed the music for the Dublin Special
    Olympics.

4   Matthew Dubourg **(b. 1707–67)**
    A violinist, conductor and composer, Dubourg led the orchestra at the premiere of
    Handel's *Messiah* at the New Music Hall in Dublin on 13 April 1742.

5   John Field **(b. Dublin; 1782–1837)**
    He wrote seven piano concertos and a series of chamber compositions for piano and
    strings, but he is chiefly remembered as the 'Father of the Nocturne'*.

6   Paddy Heeney **(b. Dublin; 1881–1911)**
    Heeney composed the music to the Irish national anthem, 'Amhrán na bhFiann' ('The
    Soldier's Song').

7   Dónal Lunny **(b. Newbridge, Co. Kildare; 1947–)**
    He is a traditional musician who has introduced a variety of new instruments and styles
    into the traditional genre.

8   Thomas Moore (b. Dublin; 1779–1852)
     This poet, singer, songwriter and entertainer is most well known for 'The Minstrel Boy'
     and 'The Last Rose of Summer'. (John Stevenson (1761–1833) composed the music for
     the latter.)

9   Seán Ó Ríada (b. Cork; 1931–71)
     Ó Ríada was the composer of 'Mise Éire', a mass in the sean-nós singing tradition, and he
     composed music for The Chieftains.

10   Bill Whelan (b. Limerick; 1950–)
     A short piece that he composed for the interval of the 1994 Eurovision Song Contest enti-
     tled *Riverdance* was accompanied by traditional Irish dancing. This performance led to the
     full-length show of the same name.

     * A nocturne is a short composition of a romantic nature

TOP 10
MOST EXPENSIVE PAINTINGS BY IRISH ARTISTS

1 Francis Bacon (1909–92) *Triptych 1976*
$86.3 million at Sotheby's, New York, 14 May 2008

2 Francis Bacon (1909–92) *Study From Innocent X*
$52.6 million at Sotheby's, New York, 15 May 2007

3 William Orpen (1878–1931) *Portrait of Gardenia St George With Riding Crop*
£1,983,500 at Sotheby's, London, 18 May 2001

4 Jack Butler Yeats RHA (1871–1957) *The Whistle of a Jacket*
£1.4 million at Christie's, London, 17 May 2001

5 John Lavery (1856–1941) *The Bridge at Grez*
£1,321,500 at Christie's, London, 8 December 1998

6 Louis le Brocquy (1916–) *Travelling Woman with Newspaper*
£1,158,500 at Sotheby's, London, 18 May 2000

7 William Scott OBE RA (1913–89) *Bowl, Eggs and Lemons*
£1,071,650 at Christie's, London, 6 June 2008

8 James Barry RA (1741–1806) *King Lear Weeping Over the Body of Cordelia*
£982,400 at Sotheby's, London, May 2006

9 Roderic O'Conor (1860–1940) *La Lisiere Du Bois*
£792,000 at Sotheby's, London, 13 May 2005

10 Walter Frederick Osborne (1859–1903) *In the Garden, Castlewood Avenue*
€825,330 at Adams, Dublin, 5 December 2001

TOP10 PAINTERS

1 **Francis Bacon (b. Dublin; 1909–92)**
Bacon was a figurative painter noted for bleak observations of the human condition.

2 **Robert Barker (b. Kells, Co. Meath; 1739–1806)**
He was the first artist to use the term 'panorama'. Barker used it to describe his paintings of Edinburgh, which were on a cylindrical surface.

3 **James Barry (b. Cork; 1741–1806)**
Barry was the most important of the Irish neoclassical artists.

4 **Louis le Brocquy (b. Dublin; 1916–)**
He is the only living painter to be included in the Permanent Irish Collection of the National Gallery of Ireland and was the first living person after President Douglas Hyde to be depicted on a postage stamp.

5 **Harold Clarke (b. Dublin; 1889–1931)**
Clarke was an illustrator and stained-glass artist. One of his signature stained-glass works is a window illustrating John Keats's 'The Eve of St Agnes' in the Hugh Lane Municipal Gallery in Dublin.

6 **Letitia Hamilton (b. Dunboyne, Co. Meath; 1878–1964)**
An Impressionist, Hamilton won the Olympic Games Art Section bronze medal for painting in London in 1948.

7 **Roderic O'Conor (b. Roscommon; 1860–1940)**
Impressionist Roderic O'Conor was a friend of Gauguin's. O'Conor's work is characterized by the use of bold colours and contrasting colour combinations.

8 **William Orpen (b. Stillorgan, Dublin; 1878–1931)**
Orpen was the leading society portraitist of his time.

9 **Walter Frederick Osborne (b. Rathmines, Dublin; 1859–1903)**
One of the most respected Irish Impressionists, Osborne painted women, children and the elderly as well as rural scenes.

10 **Jack Butler Yeats (b. London; 1871–1957)**
Brother of the poet William Butler Yeats, Jack was an illustrator and oil painter. Alongside Bacon, he was the most important Irish artist of the 20th century.

ANCIENT LITERARY CHARACTERS WHO MAY NOT HAVE EXISTED

1   **Conchóbhar mac Nessa**
    An Ulster king who enjoyed halcyon reign at Eamhain Mhacha during the stories of the
    Ulster Cycle.

2   **Conn Céadchathach (of the Hundred Battles)**
    In English, his name means 'Conn of the Hundred Battles'. He was an ancestor of the
    Connachta, who took control of the Boyne Valley in the 4th century.

3   **Cormac Mac Áirt**
    King of Ireland from AD 227–266, he was depicted as a wise, Solomon-like king in stories
    borrowed from European sources.

4   **Cúchulainn**
    Cúchulainn was the leader of a Louth-based warrior cult, probably related to Setantii or
    Belgae (his first name was Setanta and his spear 'Gae Bolga'.) 'Cu' was a common designa-
    tion for a warrior in the 8th century when stories of Cúchulainn first appear. He was given
    the role of defending Ulster single-handed against the army of Connacht.

5   Deirdre
The best-known figure from **Celtic mythology, she eloped with** Naoíse, fleeing across
Ireland with the king of Ulster **in pursuit. Conchobar tricked her i**nto returning and killed
her husband, bringing about **her eventual suicide.**

6   Díarmait Ua Duibhne
This legendary figure possessed **a love mark that made him irresisti**ble to women. When he
eloped with Fionn's betrothe**d, Gráinne, they were pursued all** over Ireland for years, until
Díarmait was gored by a boar **and allowed to die by Fionn.**

7   Eógan Mór (also known **as Mug Nuadat)**
The founding king of Munster, **he was the husband of Béara, the** Castilian princess, for
whom the Beara Peninsula is **named. His fairy mistress was Étaín** of Inis Grecraige.

8   Fionn MacCumhaill
A seer who was attached to a **warrior cult in Allen, Co. Kildare, wh**o were seeking to regain
possession of the Boyne Valley **in the 6th century. Within 200** years a body of stories
became attached to him as leade**r of a mythical band, the Fianna.**

9   Níall Noigíallach
In English his name means 'N**iall of the Nine Hostages'. He suppose**dly took hostages from
each of the different provinces **of Ireland, as well as from the** Scots, Saxons, British and
French. An ancestor of the Uí N**éill, he dominated the high king**ship for six centuries. He
was said to have flourished **in the early 5th century but was** first mentioned in the
9th century.

10   Oisín
The son of Fionn MacCumha**ill, he sojourned in the land of** youth, Tír na nÓg, with the
beautiful Niamh after the collap**se of the Fianna at Cáth Gabhra** and returned to be converted by St Patrick. He is bare**ly mentioned until the 12th-century** *Acallam na Senórach*.
His son Oscar, the bravest **of the Fianna, does not appear in** Fenian literature until the
11th century.

10

HYMNS BY IRISH WRITERS

1   'Abide with Me' Henry Lyte (1793–1847)
    Lyte was born in England but educated at Portora Royal School, Enniskillen, and Trinity
    College, Dublin. His first curacy was at Taghmon, Co. Wexford. He also wrote 'Praise My
    Soul the King of Heaven'.

2   'All Things Bright and Beautiful' Cecil Alexander (1818–95)
    Born in Dublin and raised in Wicklow, Alexander married clergyman William Alexander
    in 1850. He eventually became the Bishop of Derry. Her *Hymns for Little Children* (1848)
    went into 69 editions. She also wrote 'There is a Green Hill Far Away'.

3   'Blessed Quietness' Manie Ferguson (1850–1932)
    She spent much of her life in the USA, but Manie Ferguson (née Payne) was born in
    Carlow. She founded the Peniel Mission in Los Angeles with her husband.

4   'Jesus, Immortal King, Arise' Aaron Seymour (1789–1870)
    The son of an English clergyman, Seymour was born in Co. Limerick.

5   'Jesus, Stand Among Us' William Pennefather (1816–73)
    Pennefather was born in Dublin. After graduating from Trinity College in 1840, he took
    Holy Orders in 1841.

6   'Rock Of Ages' Augustus Toplady (1740–78)
    English-born Toplady moved to Ireland in 1755 with his mother after the death of his
    Irish-born father in 1741. Shortly after arriving in Ireland he underwent a religious
    conversion after listening to a Methodist sermon at Ballynaslaney, Co. Wexford.

7   'Sweet the Moments, Rich in Blessing' Walter Shirley (1725–86)
    Shirley was for some time Rector of Loughrea, Co. Galway.

8   'The Inheritance of the Saints' William Urwick (1791–1868)
Born in Dublin, Urwick was ordained to the ministry at Sligo.

9   'With Gladsome Feet We Press' Robert Corbet Singleton
(1810–81)
Singleton was born in Aclare, Co. Meath. In 1868 he co-edited *The Anglican Hymn-Book*,
which contained the above work.

10 'Worship The Lord in the Beauty of Holiness' John Monsell
(1811–75)
Born in Derry, he also wrote 'Fight The Good Fight With All Thy Might'.

10

PHILOSOPHERS

1   George Berkeley (b. Kilkenny; 1685–1753)
    This theologian and bishop coined the phrase 'To be is to be perceived'.

2   Edmund Burke (b. Dublin; 1729–97)
    Raised in Cork, Burke is remembered for his opposition to the French Revolution and is
    viewed as the philosophical founder of modern conservatism.

3   Anna Doyle Wheeler (b. Fennor, Co Tipperary; 1785–1848)
    Wheeler was a feminist philosopher and she shared her ideas on her travels between
    London, Dublin and Caen. William Thompson credits many of the ideas in *Appeal of One
    Half of the Human Race*, written in 1825, to her.

4   Johannes Scotus Eriugena (*c*.815–77)
    Eriugena was director of the Palatine Academy at the court of King Charles the Bald and
    was responsible for a revival of philosophical thought in Europe.

5   William Graham (b. Saintfield, Co. Down; 1840–1910)
    His book *The Creed of Science*, written in 1881, reconciled new theories of energy, evolution
    and natural selection with old religious beliefs.

6   Francis Hutcheson (b. Saintfield, Co. Down; 1694–1746)
    Hutcheson argued that providence had made provision for the happiness of the human
    race: 'That action is best which procures the greatest happiness for the greatest numbers.'

7   Dorothy King-Durie (b. Dublin; 1613–64)
    Durie was an advocate of education for women.

8   William Molyneux (b. Dublin; 1656–98)
    This political theorist's writings on Irish parliamentary rights helped inspire the American
    Revolution.

9   John Toland (b. Innishowen; 1670–1722)
    Toland wrote about political and religious philosophy in particular. He criticized blind
    faith in his controversial and influential *Christianity Not Mysterious*, written in 1696.

10 Richard Whately (b. London; 1787–1863)
    Whately served as Archbishop of Dublin from 1831–63. He was the first major Anglican
    churchman to embrace secular social sciences. He wrote, 'He only is exempt from failures
    who makes no efforts'.

ENTERTAINMENT

10 ENTERTAINERS YOU MIGHT NOT RECOGNIZE

	Real name	Better known as
1	Ronald Cleghorn	Ronnie Carroll
2	Patrick Andrew Cusack	Pete Briquette
3	David Evans	The Edge
4	Paul Hewson	Bono
5	Ciaran Morrison and Mick O'Hara	Zig and Zag
6	Johnny Morrison	Dustin the Turkey
7	Raymond Edward O'Sullivan	Gilbert O'Sullivan
8	Rosemary Scallon	Dana
9	Sean Sherrard	Johnny Logan
10	William Shields	Barry Fitzgerald

TRADITIONAL SINGERS

	Singer	Signature tune
1	Margaret Barry	'My Lagan Love'
2	Dominic Behan	'The Patriot Game'
3	Mary Black	'No Frontiers'
4	Dolores Keane	'Rambling Irishman'
5	Peadar Kearney	'Amhrán na bhFiann' ('The Soldier's Song')
6	Tommy Makem	'Four Green Fields'
7	Christy Moore	'Lisdoonvarna'
8	Delia Murphy	'Galway Shawl'
9	Nioclás Tóibín	'Roisin Dubh'
10	Paddy Tunney	'The Lark in the Morning'

10
TRADITIONAL MUSICIANS

1 Liam Clancy (b. Carrick-on-Suir, Co. Tipperary; 1935–2009)
   Liam was the youngest of a Carrick-on-Suir musical family that shot to prominence after
   an unprecedented 16-minute slot on *The Ed Sullivan Show* in 1961.

2 Willie Clancy (b. Miltown Malbay, Co. Clare; 1918–73)
   He was a piper at the heart of the 1960s piping revival. His life and work have been
   commemorated by a summer school in his hometown.

3 Michael Coleman (b. nr Ballymote, Co. Sligo; 1891–1946)
   This fiddler settled in New York in 1914. His ornate style on a series of 78 rpm records in
   the 1920s and 1930s helped popularize fiddle music.

4 Thomas Connellan (b. Cloonmahon, Co. Sligo; 1645–98)
   Connellan was a harper who composed 'Fáinne Geal an Lae' ('The Dawning of the Day').

5 Séamus Ennis (b. Jamestown, North Co. Dublin; 1919–82)
   This piper, folk-song collector and co-founder of the Piobairi Uileann (Society of Irish
   Pipers) helped revive the piping tradition in the 1950s.

6 Cornelius Lyons (b. Macroom, Co. Cork; *c.*1670–1750)
   This harper is best remembered for his interpretation of a number of tunes including 'The
   Coolin', 'Eileen A Roone' and 'What Is That to Him'.

7 Turlough O' Carolan (b. Nobber, Co. Meath; 1670–1738)
   O'Carolan was a blind harper who introduced flourishes from Italian composers, such as
   Verdi, into traditional Irish music.

8 Donnchadh Ó Hámsaigh (b. Garvagh, Co. Derry; 1695–1807)
   He was the oldest performer at the 1792 Belfast Harp Festival and the only harper there
   who employed the traditional fingernail techniques that give the Gaelic wire-strung harp
   its full range of expression. Donnchadh Ó Hámsaigh's 18th-century 'Downhill Harp' is
   now owned and displayed by the Guinness Brewery in Dublin.

9   Micho Russell (b. Doolin, Co. Clare; 1915–94)
     This tune-line tin-whistle player adopted the push and pull concertina style to the tin
     whistle. He toured Europe and America but was most at home in Gussie O'Connor's pub
     in Doolin.

10   John Scott (b. Co. Westmeath; *c.*1620–*c.*80)
     This harper is praised as the father of the *caoinan* or dirge. He composed lamentations for
     Purcell of Loughmoe and O'Hussey of Galtrim.

10 FAMOUS MELODIES

1 **'Auld Triangle'**
This song was attributed to Brendan Behan in his play *The Quare Fellow*, in 1954, but according to Frank Harte it was composed by Paddy Deegan from Islandbridge.

2 **'The Coolin'**
Associated with Cornelius Lyons (*c.*1670–1750), collector Francis 'Chief' O'Neill called it the 'queen of Irish airs'.

3 **'Danny Boy'**
The melody is close to a tune by Donnchadh Ó Hámsaigh but it is actually an English drawing-room song that was collected by Jane Ross from Limavady in 1851. It was published in 1855 and the words added by Frederic Weatherly in 1881.

4 **'Fields of Athenry'**
Written by Pete St John in 1979, it became a sports anthem for Galway, Glasgow Celtic, Irish, Munster and Liverpool fans.

5 **'Lillibullero'**
This Williamite song composed in 1689 was by Thomas Wharton and Henry Purcell based on the quotation 'an lile ba leir leo' and was used during the War of the Three Kings. It became a theme tune of the BBC's World Service in 1932.

6 **'Minstrel Boy'**
Thomas Moore's 1798 composition became popular during the American Civil War.

7 **'Rose of Tralee'**
William Mulchinock's 1849 poem, arranged by Charles Glover in 1912 and popularized by John McCormack, gave its name to a beauty pageant.

8 **'Sally Gardens'**
W. B. Yeats wrote the words to replace a more raunchy version in 1889 and it was adapted by Herbert Hughes in 1909.

9 **'The Sash My Father Wore'**
This 1850s song, printed in 1876 and associated with the Orange Order revival of the 1880s, replaced even more virulently anti-Catholic songs.

10 **'She Moved Through the Fair'**
Published by Pádraic Colum and Herbert Hughes in 1909, the song was popularized by John McCormack.

MODERN SONGWRITERS*

	Songwriter	Signature song
1	Luka Bloom	'City of Chicago'
2	Paul Brady	'The Island'
3	Paddy Casey	'Saints and Sinners'
4	Glen Hansard	'Falling Slowly'
5	Jimmy MacCarthy	'Ride On'
6	Mickey McConnell	'Only Our Rivers Run Free'
7	Shane McGowan	'Fairytale of New York'
8	Mundy (Edmund Enright)	'July'
9	Damien Rice	'9 Crimes'
10	Pete St John	'Fields of Athenry'

* All born post-1945

10 PHRASES YOU'LL NEED TO WRITE YOUR OWN IRISH BALLAD

1   All in the merry/pleasant month of (insert month, usually May – have you ever tried to find anything to rhyme with February?)

2   As I roved out

3   Carry me over

4   Come all ye

5   Come list to what I say

6   Her/his beauty was (insert)

7   My name it is (insert)

8   She/he stole my heart away

9   She met a soldier/sailor/jolly ploughboy

10   'Twas on a bright (insert month) morning

	Winner	Category	Film	Year
1	Michèle Burke (shared)	Best Make-up	*Quest for Fire*	1982
2	Daniel Day Lewis	Best Actor	*My Left Foot*	1989
3	Barry Fitzgerald	Best Supporting Actor	*Going My Way*	1945
4	Brenda Fricker	Best Supporting Actress	*My Left Foot*	1989
5	Cedric Gibbons	Best Art Direction	*Pride and Prejudice*	1940
6	Glen Hansard	Best Achievement in Music Written for Motion Pictures, Original Song	*Once*	2007
7	Neil Jordan	Best Screenplay Written Directly for the Screen	*The Crying Game*	1992
8	Josie McAvin (shared)	Best Art Direction – Set Direction	*Out of Africa*	1985
9	Martin McDonagh	Best Short Film, Live Action	*Six Shooter*	2005
10	George Bernard Shaw	Best Screenplay	*Pygmalion*	1938

Barry Fitzgerald is the only actor to have been nominated for both Best Actor and Best Supporting Actor Oscars for the same role. The rules were subsequently changed to prevent this happening again.

10 FILM ACTORS

	Name	Where born	Year
1	Kenneth Branagh	Downview, Co. Antrim	1960
2	Pierce Brosnan	Navan, Co. Meath	1953
3	Gabriel Byrne	Dublin	1950
4	Colin Farrell	Castleknock, Dublin	1976
5	Brendan Gleeson	Dublin	1955
6	Richard Harris	Limerick	1930
7	Colm Meaney	Dublin	1953
8	Cillian Murphy	Douglas, Co. Cork	1976
9	Liam Neeson	Ballymena, Co. Antrim	1952
10	Stephen Rea	Belfast	1946

Richard Harris died in 2002.

Peter O'Toole is often included in lists of Irish film actors as one of his two birth certificates says that he was born in Connemara, Co. Galway. The other says that he was born in Leeds.

	Name	Where	Born	Died
1	Eamon Keane	Listowel, Co. Kerry	1925	1990
2	Micheál MacLíammóir	London	1899	1978
3	Ray McAnally	Buncrana, Co. Donegal	1926	1989
4	Siobhán McKenna	Belfast	1923	1986
5	Tom Murphy	Salisbury, Rhodesia (now Harare, Zimbabwe)	1968	2007
6	Brían O'Byrne	Co. Cavan	1967	–
7	Jimmy O'Dea	Dublin	1899	1965
8	Milo O'Shea	Dublin	1926	–
9	Maureen Potter	Dublin	1925	2004
10	Noel Purcell	Dublin	1900	1985

Micheál MacLíammóir was born Alfred Willmore in London, England. He travelled around Europe in the 1920s, but decided to stay in Dublin and immerse himself in the Irish way of life. He and partner Hilton Edwards (1903–82) were co-founders of the Gate Theatre in Dublin in 1928.

Brían O'Byrne won a Tony award for his role as a serial killer in *Frozen*.

Songwriter Leo Maguire composed 'The Dublin Saunter' for Noel Purcell.

10 COMEDIANS

Name	Where born	Date of birth
1	Ed Byrne	Swords, Co. Fingal	1972
2	Neil Delamere	Edenderry, Co. Offaly	1980
3	Pauline McLynn	Sligo	1962
4	Dermot Morgan	Dublin	1952
5	Graham Norton	Clondalkin, Co. Dublin	1963
6	Dara Ó Briain	Bray, Co. Wicklow	1972
7	Ardal O'Hanlon	Carrickmacross, Co. Monaghan	1965
8	Pat Shortt	Thurles, Co. Tipperary	1966
9	Tommy Tiernan	Carndonagh, Co. Donegal	1969
10	Niall Tóibín	Cork	1929

Dermot Morgan died in 1998.

FILM DIRECTORS

	Name	Example of their work	Year released
1	Patrick Carey	*The Living Stone*	1958
2	John Carney	*Once*	2006
3	John Crowley	*Intermission*	2003
4	Rex Ingram	*Ben-Hur*	1925
5	Neil Jordan	*The Crying Game*	1992
6	Kevin McClory	*Never Say Never Again*	1983
7	John Moore	*Behind Enemy Lines*	2001
8	Pat O'Connor	*Dancing at Lughansa*	1998
9	Damien O'Donnell	*East is East*	1999
10	Jim Sheridan	*In America*	2002

BEST FILMS*

	Film	Director	Year released
1	*The Commitments*	Alan Parker	1991
2	*My Left Foot*	Jim Sheridan	1989
3	*In the Name of the Father*	Jim Sheridan	1993
4	*The Quiet Man*	John Ford	1952
5	*The Snapper*	Stephen Frears	1993
6	*Michael Collins*	Neil Jordan	1996
7	*The Field*	Jim Sheridan	1990
8	*Intermission*	John Crowley	2003
9	*Veronica Guerin*	Joel Schumacher	2003
10	*Inside I'm Dancing*	Damien O'Donnell	2004

* As voted for in 2005 in a poll by Jameson Whiskey

MOVIES FILMED IN IRELAND

	Film	Director	Year released
1	*A Lad from Old Ireland*	Sidney Olcott	1910
2	*Angela's Ashes*	Alan Parker	1999
3	*Braveheart*	Mel Gibson	1995
4	*Educating Rita*	Lewis Gilbert	1983
5	*Excalibur*	John Boorman	1981
6	*King Arthur*	Antoine Fuqua	2004
7	*Reefer and the Model*	Joe Comerford	1987
8	*Reign of Fire*	Rob Bowman	2002
9	*The Wind That Shakes the Barley*	Ken Loach	2006
10	*Widow's Peak*	John Irvin	1994

A Lad from Old Ireland was advertised as 'The first ever film recorded on two continents'. The plot involves a boy who travels from Ireland to America to 'make good'.

10 BANNED MOVIES

	Film	Director	Year released
1	*A Clockwork Orange*	Stanley Kubrick	1971
2	*From Dusk Till Dawn*	Robert Rodriguez	1996
3	*Meet the Feebles*	Peter Jackson	1989
4	*Monkey Business*	Norman Z. McLeod	1931
5	*Monty Python's Life of Brian*	Terry Jones	1979
6	*Monty Python's The Meaning of Life*	Terry Jones/ Terry Gilliam	1983
7	*Natural Born Killers*	Oliver Stone	1994
8	*Rocky Road to Dublin*	Peter Lennon	1968
9	*The Great Dictator*	Charles Chaplin	1940
10	*Ulysses*	Joseph Strick	1967

TOP 10

TV PROGRAMMES*

	Programme	Number of viewers
1	*The Late Late Toy Show*	1,199,000
2	*Nine O'Clock News*	784,000
3	*Prime Time Investigates*	773,000
4	*Killinaskully*	757,000
5	*Fair City*	715,000
6	*Buyer Beware*	714,000
7	*All-Ireland hurling final*	709,000
8	*All-Ireland football final*	703,000
9	*The Rose of Tralee*	696,000
10	*Eurovision Song Contest*	691,000

* Figures for 2008

10

QUOTES FROM *FATHER TED*

1   'I'm not a fascist. I'm a priest. Fascists dress up in black and tell people what to do.' Father Ted

2   'Won't you have some cake, Father? It's got cocaine in it. Oh no, hang on, it's not cocaine, is it? What do I mean now? The little things. Raisins!' Mrs Doyle

3   'Sorry, Ted. I was concentrating too hard on looking holy.' Father Dougal

4   'They've taken the roads in.' Father Ted

5   'I'm no good at judging the size of crowds Ted, but I'd say there's about 17 million of them out there.' Father Dougal

6   'You do like pheasant, don't you, Father? Well there's a little clue. The thing you'll be eating likes pheasant as well.' Mrs Doyle

7   'Dougal, how did you get into the Church in the first place? Was it, like, collect 12 crisp packets and become a priest?' Father Ted

8   'God, I've heard about those cults, Ted. People dressing up in black and saying Our Lord's going to come back and save us all.' Father Dougal

9   'How come all the rocks are different sizes?' Father Dougal

10   'Sheep, like all wool-bearing animals, instinctively travel north, where it's colder, and they won't be so stuffy.' Father Ted

Father Ted was televised in the mid-1990s. The series was about a trio of dysfunctional priests on an island exile off the west coast. It was written by Arthur Mathews and Graham Linehan and featured a cast of four leading comedians: Dermot Morgan from Dublin, Ardal O'Hanlon from Co. Monaghan, Frank Kelly from Dún Laoghaire and Pauline McLynn, originally from Sligo. Most of the other major Irish comedians of the time featured in at least one episode.

IRISH REFERENCES IN
THE SIMPSONS

Episode

1   'Trash of the Titans'
    Homer tries to get into a U2 concert.

2   *The Simpsons Movie*
    Lisa's crush in *The Simpsons Movie*, Colin, is the son of an Irish musician. Lisa says, 'Is he...?'
    Colin replies, 'He's not Bono.'

3   'Bart's Inner Child'
    Grampa says he chased the Irish out in 1904. An Irishman replies, 'And a fine job you
    did, too.'

4   'Homer vs. The Eighteenth Amendment'
    Moe has a 'Help Wanted: No Irish Need Apply' sign over the door.

5   'Treehouse of Horror XII'
    Marge buys a computer called the Ultrahouse, which runs the household. She chooses for
    it to have the voice of Pierce Brosnan.

6   'Homer vs. The Eighteenth Amendment'
    One of the floats in the Springfield St Patrick's Day parade is the 'Drunken Irish Novelists
    of Springfield'.

7   'Whacking Day'
    Bart says that Springfield's Snake Whacking Day was made up as an excuse to beat up the
    Irish. An Irishman says, 'But 'twas all in good fun.'

8   'Last Exit to Springfield'
    Springfield Nuclear Power Plant's trade union puts a clause in a contract that every
    employee should get a green cookie on St Patrick's Day.

9   'Who Shot Mr Burns? Part Two'
    Smithers says he tried to march in the New York St Patrick's Day parade.

10 'In the Name of the Grandfather'
    The entire episode is set in Ireland. The family take Grampa for one last drink at his
    favourite bar, O'Flanagan's.

FAMOUS ADVERTISING CAMPAIGNS

	Campaign	Product/Company	Year
1	Jim Figgerty	Jacobs' Fig Rolls	1968
2	Barney and Beany	Bachelors beans	1971
3	Safe Cross Code	Road safety	1971
4	Look up it's Aer Lingus	Aer Lingus	1975
5	*Tá siad ag teacht*	Guinness	1977
6	Sally O'Brien 'and the way she might look at you'	Harp lager	1980
7	'Marino Waltz'	Bord na Móna peat briquettes	1983
8	The fillet of cheddar	Kilmeaden cheese	1983
9	Dancing Man	Guinness	1994
10	Quarrel	Guinness	2003

Judge, from the popular children's show *Wanderly Wagon*, was the narrator of the Safe Cross Code ad.

Sally O'Brien in the Harp lager ad was played by Vicki Michelle, who starred in *'Allo, 'Allo!* as Yvette Carte-Blanche.

FIRST PROGRAMMES
SHOWN ON RTÉ

1 *At Home and Abroad*
A programme for younger viewers presented by Seán Mac Réamoinn.

2 *Buckskin: The Outlaw's Boy*
Starring Tom Nolan, this was a Western series about the adventures of a boy in the frontier town of Buckskin.

3 *Siopa an Breathnaigh*
A weekly serial about the Irish-speaking Breathnach family. It was written by Niall Tóibín, and starred Kevin Flood, Ronnie Masterson, Brendan Cauldwell, Eoin Mac Aogáin, Clorinda Holland, Mark Callan and Fergus Cogley.

4 *Bachelor Father*
This comedy series starred John Forsythe and was about an unwed father who lived in a house with his young niece and Chinese manservant. The episode was entitled 'Peter Meets His Match'.

5 *Broadsheet*
John O'Donoghue introduced Ireland's nightly review of people and events.

6 *The Aquanauts*
An underwater adventure series.

7 *For Your Pleasure*
A music programme featuring Sean Bracken's Loch Ghamhna Ceili Band.

8 *Dragnet*
A series based on the records of the Los Angeles Police Department.

9 *Mackenzie's Raiders*
This American Western series was based on the exploits of the fourth cavalry on the Mexican border.

10 *On the Land*
A weekly programme for Irish farmers introduced by Patrick Jennings.

RTÉ started broadcasting on 1 January 1962.

FIRSTS FOR IRISH RADIO

1 **17 October 1907**
   Guglielmo Marconi, whose mother and wife were both Irish, established the first commercial transatlantic radio communications service, between Clifden, Co. Galway, and Glace Bay, Newfoundland, Canada.

2 **24 May 1926**
   The first advertised news bulletin was broadcast on 2RN.

3 **29 August 1926**
   The All-Ireland hurling semi-final between Kilkenny and Galway was commentated on by Cork-born sportswriter Paddy Mehigan. It was the first sports commentary broadcast outside of the USA.

4 **10 March 1927**
   Mairéad Ní Ghráda was appointed 2RN's Woman Organizer, responsible for women's and children's programmes. She produced the first children's programme on the station, *Uair i dTír na nÓg*, which featured Molly Shillman, Lillian Brooks and Harry O'Dempsey.

5 **26 June 1929**
   The first broadcast of a horse race, the Irish Derby, took place.

6 **1 September 1929**
   The radio engineer was locked out of the All-Ireland hurling final by GAA president Sean Ryan. Ryan was worried that the broadcast would affect the match attendance.

7 **15 June 1936**
   A tour of Dublin Zoo was broadcast live. The sounds were sometimes indistinct but the 'one distinctive sound that came over was from the laughing hyena'.

8 **20 February 1937**
   The first and only live broadcast of a bridge international took place. It was Ireland vs. Scotland from the Shelbourne Hotel in Dublin.

9 **5 September 1937**
   Technical problems at the All-Ireland hurling final in Killarney meant that the two commentators and Seán Óg Ó Ceallacháin had to take notes of the match and then rush to the post office to give a commentary 'as live'.

10 **6 September 1953**
   The first relayed broadcast from Ireland on shortwave to Radio Brazzaville in the Congo.

WORDS AND LANGUAGE

10 WORDS INVENTED IN IRELAND

1   **Bard**
From *bard*, meaning 'poet'.

2   **Bog**
From the Irish word for 'soft'.

3   **Boycott**
From 'Captain Boycott', 19th-century evicting landlord.

4   **Brogue**
From *bróg*, meaning 'shoe'.

5   **Callow**
From the Irish for 'bald', *caladh*.

6   **Galore**
From *go leor*, meaning 'sufficiency'.

7   **Glen**
From *glean*, a 'valley'.

8   **Loch**
From *loch*, a 'lake'.

9   **Tory**
Originally it was a deprecating term for an Irish outlaw, from *tóir*, the verb 'to pursue'. It was later used to refer to English Jacobite supporters and eventually adopted as a badge of honour by English Conservatives.

10 **Whiskey**
From *uisce beatha*, 'water of life'.

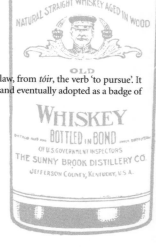

PHRASES FROM THE IRISH LANGUAGE

Irish	English
1	*B'fhéidir*	Maybe
2	*Buíochas le Dia*	Thank God
3	*Gabh mo leithscéal*	Excuse me
4	*Go raibh maith agat*	Thank you
5	*Is dóigh liom*	I suppose
6	*Maith go leor*	OK
7	*Mas é do thoil é*	Please
8	*Sláinte*	Your health (a toast)
9	*Slán leat*	Goodbye
10	*Tá fáilte romhat*	You are welcome

10 ENGLISH WORDS DERIVED FROM THE IRISH LANGUAGE

	English	Irish derivation
1	Jockey	*Jachaí*, a horseman
2	Phoney	*Fáinne*, a confidence trick involving a ring
3	Plaid	*Pluid*, a blanket
4	Shanty	*Sean ti*, an old house
5	Shebeen	*Síbín*, a mugful
6	Slew	*Slua*, a lot
7	Slogan	*Gairm slógaidh*, a battle cry
8	Smithereen	*Smidrín*, a small particle
9	Trousers	*Tríusas*, originally a distinguishing garment of Ireland
10	Truant	*Truaghan*, a wretch

WORDS IN ULSTER SCOTS

Ulster Scots	English
1 *Danner*	Stroll
2 *Dicht*	Wipe
3 *Gulder*	Shout
4 *Kye*	Cattle
5 *Nor*	Than
6 *Ocht*	Anything
7 *Sheuch*	Ditch
8 *Thran*	Awkward
9 *Wheen*	Several
10 *Whiles*	Sometimes

Ulster Scots, or Ullans, is spoken by about 35,000 people in the north of Ireland. Although treated as a dialect of English it has many distinctive words.

10 WORDS IN SHELTA

Shelta	English
1	*Akhonshk*	Today
2	*Byohr*	Woman
3	*Goikhera*	Infant
4	*Gris*	Charm
5	*Noos a Daalyon*	God's grace
6	*Shaykar*	Sister
7	*Sinawl*	Beer
8	*Thoaber*	Road
9	*Thoamaan*	A lot
10	*Yoarum*	Milk

Shelta, also known as Caintíotar, Gammen, Pavee, Sheldru or the Cant, is the language of the Travelling community and is still spoken by an estimated 80,000 people. Words feature in the lyrics of The Saw Doctors' songs and in provincial town dialect.

WORDS IN YOLA

Yola	English
1 Caule	Horse
2 Earnough	Hilarious
3 Graapish	Stale meat
4 Houghany	Stupid
5 Klouk	Awkward woman
6 Pomeale	Fool
7 Rusheen	Snack
8 Shaamfast	Bashful
9 Trameal	Lazy person
10 Unket	Shy

The last native speaker of the Yola language, spoken almost exclusively in south-west Wexford, Martin Parle died in 1870. The above words were chosen from the only glossary of Yola, a list of 1,700 words and phrases compiled by Jacob Poole in 1827 and published in 1867. The extinct language of north Dublin, Fingallian, may have had a similar vocabulary.

PHRASES IN YOLA

Yola	English
1 *Lhause a dher*	Open the door
2 *Theene a dher*	Close the door
3 *Yer hele!*	Your health!
4 *Hele an greve apa thee!*	Health and wealth to you!
5 *Faade teit thee – zo lournagh?*	What ails you, you're so sad?
6 *Zo wough kisth an wough parthet*	So we kissed and we parted
7 *Aar's no gazb in him*	There's not a breath of life in him
8 *Aar's a dole o'sneow apa greoune to die*	There's a lot of snow on the ground today
9 *Aar's dhurth a heighe*	There's dirty weather above
10 *Caules will na get to wullow to die*	Horses won't be able to tumble today

THE FAMOUS AND
INFAMOUS

10
OSCAR WILDE ONE-LINERS

1   'Always forgive your enemies – nothing annoys them so much.'

2   'Education is an admirable thing, but it is well to remember from time to time that nothing that is worth knowing can be taught.'

3   'Every woman is a rebel, and usually in wild revolt against herself.'

4   'Only dull people are brilliant at breakfast.'

5   'Moderation is a fatal thing – nothing succeeds like excess.'

6   'Nothing spoils a romance so much as a sense of humour in a woman – or the lack of it in a man.'

7   'The old believe everything, the middle-aged suspect everything, the young know everything.'

8   .'To love oneself is the beginning of a lifelong romance.'

9   'Woman begins by resisting a man's advances and ends by blocking his retreat.'

10 'Young men want to be faithful, and are not; old men want to be faithless and are not.'

Oscar Fingal O'Flahertie Wills Wilde (1854–1900) was born at 21 Westland Row, Dublin. He was educated at Portora, Trinity College Dublin and Oxford. Wilde was an early advocate of 'art for art's sake' in his only novel, *The Picture of Dorian Gray*, published in 1890. He achieved success as a comic dramatist with *Lady Windermere's Fan*, published in 1892, and *The Importance of Being Earnest*, published in 1895. His life then took a dramatic turn when he was imprisoned for homosexual offences in Reading jail from 1895–7; he died in exile in Paris.

FAMOUS PEOPLE AND THE AGES AT WHICH THEY DIED

	Name	What known for	Died	Age
1	Kevin Barry	Revolutionary	1 Nov 1920	18
2	Robert Emmet	Orator and patriot	20 Sept 1803	25
3	Sarah Curran	Girlfriend of Robert Emmet	5 May 1808	26
4	Molly Malone	Subject of famous Dublin ballad	13 Jun 1699	29
5	Francis Ledwidge	Poet	31 Jul 1917	29
6	Thomas Davis	Poet and patriot	16 Sept 1845	30
7	Michael Collins	First commander of Irish Army	22 Aug 1922	31
8	Frances 'Fanny' Parnell	Founder of Ladies Land League	20 Jul 1882	33
9	Thomas 'Buck' Whaley	Adventurer	2 Nov 1800	33
10	Lord Edward Fitzgerald	Aristocrat and revolutionary	4 Jun 1798	34

10
PEOPLE AWARDED THE FREEDOM OF DUBLIN

	Recipient	Year awarded
1	Bono	2000
2	Jack Charlton	1994
3	Bill Clinton	1995
4	Ronnie Delany	2006
5	Bob Geldof	2006
6	Kevin Heffernan	2004
7	John F. Kennedy	1963
8	Thomas Kinsella	2007
9	Nelson Mandela	1988
10	Mother Teresa	1993

In all 74 people have been given the Freedom of the City of Dublin. The award carries the right to pasture sheep on St Stephen's Green, and Bono exercised this right on the day of his ceremony.

NOBEL LAUREATES

	Name	Born	Prize	Year
1	Samuel Beckett (1906–89)	Dublin	Literature	1969
2	Betty Williams (1943–)	Belfast	Peace	1976
3	Mairead Corrigan (1944–)	Belfast	Peace	1976
4	Seamus Heaney (1939–)	Bellaghy	Literature	1995
5	John Hume (1937–)	Derry	Peace	1998
6	Seán MacBride (1904–88)	Dublin	Peace	1974
7	George Bernard Shaw (1856–1950)	Dublin	Literature	1925
8	David Trimble (1944–)	Bangor	Peace	1998
9	Ernest Walton (1903–95)	Dublin	Physics	1951
10	W. B. Yeats (1865–1939)	Dublin	Literature	1923

Betty Williams and Mairead Corrigan were co-founders of the Northern Ireland Peace Movement (later renamed Community of Peace People).

In addition to winning the Nobel Peace Prize in 1974, Seán MacBride also won the Lenin Peace Prize for 1975–76. At the time of his death he was the only person in the world to hold both prizes. He nursed the European Convention on Human Rights through the Council of Europe, and helped found and lead Amnesty International.

10 AVIATORS

1   **Richard Crosbie (1755–1800)**
Crosbie was the first Irishman to make a manned flight. On 19 January 1785 he flew from Ranelagh to Clontarf by hot air balloon.

2   **Michael Dargan (1918–2005)**
He was the first Irish president of the International Air Transport Association.

3   **James Fitzmaurice (1898–1965)**
Raised in Portlaoise, this aviation pioneer made the first successful transatlantic aircraft flight from east to west in April 1928.

4   **Alan Joyce (1966–)**
Joyce was the first Irish CEO of Qantas Airways.

5   **Michael O'Leary (1961–)**
From Mullingar, the chief executive of Ryanair built the airline up from a fleet of 40 to over 200, to become Europe's largest airline in terms of passenger numbers.

6   **Mary Pierce-Evans (1896–1939)**
Pierce-Evans set records for altitude and was the first woman to parachute from an aeroplane.

7   **Tony Ryan (1936–2007)**
From Thurles, Ryan built the largest aircraft-leasing operation in the world by the end of the 1980s, Guinness Peat Aviation, and then founded Ryanair.

8   **Richard Saul (1891–1965)**
This Dublin-born pilot became the vice-chair of the International Transport Commission in Rome.

9   **Willie Walsh (1961–)**
In October 2005 Walsh became the first Irish CEO of British Airways.

10 **Denys Corbett Wilson (1882–1915)**
Wilson set a record time for flying between the island of Great Britain and Ireland in 1912. His journey from Goodwick in Pembrokeshire, Wales, to Enniscorthy, Co. Wexford, took 1 hr 40 mins.

SURPRISING BIRTHPLACES

	Name	Occupation	Where born/Year
1	Eamon Bulfin	Revolutionary	Argentina, 1892
2	David Curtis	Rugby player	Zimbabwe, 1965
3	Chris de Burgh	Singer	Argentina, 1948
4	Jamie Heaslip	Rugby player	Tiberias, Israel, 1983
5	Seán MacBride	Revolutionary	Paris, 1904
6	David Norris	Politician	Leopoldville, Belgian Congo, 1944
7	Ronan O'Gara	Rugby player	San Diego, USA, 1977
8	Seán Óg Ó hAilpín	Hurler	Rotuma, Fiji, 1977
9	Frankie Sheahan	Rugby player	Toronto, Canada, 1976
10	Jim Whitley	Soccer player	Zambia, 1975

10
HONORARY CITIZENS

Name	Conferred
1 Alfred Chester Beatty	1957
2= Alfred Beit (and his wife Clementine)	1993
4= Jack Charlton (and his wife Pat)	1996
6= Tiede Herrema (and his wife Elisabeth)	1975
8 Derek Hill	1999
9 Jean Kennedy Smith	1998
10= Tip O'Neill (and his wife Milly)	1984

NOTABLE CENTENARIANS

	Name	What known for	Lived to
1	Gretta Bowen	Artist	101 (1880–1981)
2	Peggy Elliott	Queen of Trasna Island, Lough Erne	107 (1760–1867)
3	Catherine FitzGerald	Wife of Earl of Desmond	110 (1494–1604)
4	Mary Harris	US labour leader	100 (1830–1930)
5	Dan Keating	Veteran of War of Independence	105 (1902–2007)
6	St Kevin	Founder and first abbot of Glendalough	120 (502–622)
7	Charles Macklin	Actor	100 (1697–1797)
8	Thomas Maguire	Veteran of War of Independence/survivor of Second Dáil	101 (1892–1993)
9	Donnchadh Ó Hámsaigh	Harper	112 (1695–1807)
10	Gearóid O'Sullivan	Veteran of War of Independence/survivor of Second Dáil	103 (1891–1994)

Catherine FitzGerald reputedly died in a fall from an apple tree.

Researchers have challenged whether Mary Harris did in fact live until she was 100.

10 MEN BEHIND THE INITIALS

	Name	Stand(s) for	Dates	What known for
1	D. J. Carey	Denis Joseph	1970–	Hurler
2	W. T. Cosgrave	William Thomas	1880–1965	Taoiseach
3	Oliver J. Flanagan	Oliver James	1920–87	Politician
4	F. R. Higgins	Frederick Robert	1896–1941	Poet
5	C. S. Lewis	Clive Staples	1898–1963	Writer
6	J. P. MacManus	John Patrick	1951–	Entrepreneur
7	T. J. Maher	Thomas Joseph	1922–2002	Activist and politician
8	T. C. Murray	Thomas Cornelius	1873–1959	Playwright
9	Sean T. O'Kelly	Sean Thomas	1882–1966	President
10	P. J. Ruttledge	Patrick Joseph	1892–1952	Polititican

FAMOUS PEOPLE WHO LEFT SCHOOL EARLY

	Name	What known for	Age at which left school
1	Brendan Behan	Playwright	14
2	Eamon Dunphy	Sportswriter	13
3	Brenda Fricker	Actress	14
4	Douglas Hyde	Scholar and president	13
5	Peadar Kearney	Composer	14
6	Patrick MacGill	Writer	14
7	Sean O'Casey	Playwright	9
8	Frank Patterson	Tenor	14
9	Maureen Potter	Actress	12
10	George Bernard Shaw	Playwright	15

TALES OF SEXUAL EXPLOITS

1   Eamonn Casey (1927–)
    A staunch defender of priestly celibacy, Eamonn Casey was exposed as the father of an 18-year-old boy by his former housekeeper Annie Murphy on 5 May 1992. He was Bishop of Galway at the time the information became public.

2   Michael Cleary (d. 1993)
    Cleary was a parish priest of Ballyfermot and Ballymun, and held orthodox and conservative views on theological issues. After his death in 1993 he was revealed as the father of two children by his housekeeper Phyllis Hamilton.

3   Nellie Clifden (not known)
    From Dublin, she was an actress with whom Albert Saxe-Coburg, later King Edward VII of England, lost his virginity in September 1861.

4   Eliza Gilbert (1821–61)
    Mistress of King Ludwig I of Bavaria, this Limerick-born woman posed as 'Lola Montez', the Spanish dancer. When the local bishop reprimanded Ludwig he replied, 'You have your stola and I have my Lola.'

5   Charles Haughey (1925–2006)
    Haughey was a three-time Taoiseach from Malahide. In 1999, journalist Terry Keane went on RTÉ's *The Late Late Show* and revealed that she had been having an affair with Haughey since 1972.

6   Percy Jocelyn (1764–1843)
    This Church of Ireland bishop of Clogher was dismissed in 1822 for 'immorality, incontinence, sodomitical habits and propensities and neglect of his spiritual, judicial, and ministerial duties'. He was caught in flagrante with a soldier in a White Hart Lane tavern.

7 Dorothea Jordan (1761–1816)
This actress was the mistress of the future King William IV of England for 20 years.

8 Eliza Lynch (1835–86)
Born in Cork, she was the mistress of Francisco Solano López, the president of Paraguay.

9 Daniel O'Connell (1775–1847)
An 1832 pamphlet by an inmate in Fleet Street prison in London accused this political leader of having a child out of wedlock. This led to a series of accusations about sexual promiscuity.

10 Marie-Louise O'Morphi (1737–1814)
O'Morphi was one of Louis XV's mistresses. Having failed to become his 'official mistress' a marriage to an elderly army officer was arranged for her. He was killed in 1757. She married twice more.

10 IRISHMEN WHO NEVER MARRIED

	Name/Dates	What known for
1	Joseph Biggar (1828–90)	Politician
2	Thomas Davis (1814–45)	Poet
3	Joseph Devlin (1871–1934)	Nationalist politician
4	John Devoy (1842–1928)	Fenian
5	Barry Fitzgerald (1888–1961)	Actor
6	Oliver Goldsmith (1728–74)	Writer
7	George Moore (1852–1933)	Writer
8	John O'Leary (1830–1907)	Fenian
9	Horace Plunkett (1854–1932)	Agriculturist
10	J. M. Synge (1871–1909)	Playwright

PEOPLE FROM LARGE FAMILIES

	Name	What known for	Size of family
1	Charlotte Brooke	Writer	22
2	Christy Brown	Writer/Painter	22
3	Eibhlín Dubh ní Chonaill	Poet	22
4	Dan Donnelly	Prizefighter	17
5	Larry Dunne	Drug dealer	24
6	Augusta, Lady Gregory	Writer and dramatist	16
7	Damien Fitzhenry	Hurler	15
8	Pádraig 'Pecker' Dunne	Musician	23
9	Arthur Guinness II	Brewery owner	21
10	Anna Haslam	Suffragette	21

Christy Browne (1932–81) was the tenth of 22 children, 13 of whom survived. His account of his early life, *My Left Foot*, was made into a film in 1989 and he was played by Daniel Day Lewis.

10 PEOPLE WHO STUDIED IN IRELAND

	Name/Dates	Nationality	What known for
1	George Abbot (1562–1633)	English	Archbishop of Canterbury
2	Felipe Contepomi (1977–)	Argentinian	Rugby player
3	J. P. Donleavy (1926–)	American	Writer
4	Varahagiri Giri (1894–1980)	Indian	Trade Unionist/ Presient
5	Nada Haffadh (1957–)	Bahraini	Politician
6	William Laud (1573–1645)	English	Archbishop of Canterbury
7	Martin Sheen (1940–)	American	Actor
8	Edward Stafford (1819–1901)	Scottish	Prime Minister of New Zealand
9	Mother Teresa (1910–97)	Macedonian	Missionary
10	Jaja Wachuku (1918–96)	Nigerian	Politician/ humanitarian

Nada Haffadh studied at the Royal College of Surgeons in Dublin. She became Bahrain's first ever female cabinet minister when she was made Minister of Health in 2004. She held the position for three years.

Despite persistent rumours that Brazilian footballer Sócrates de Oliveira studied in Dublin and even played in the League of Ireland, Sócrates has stated that he has never been to Dublin.

PEOPLE WITH AN IRISH FATHER

	Name/Dates	What known for
1	Alan Brooke (1883–1963)	Chief military adviser during Second World War
2	Henry Ford (1863–1947)	Car manufacturer
3	Noel (1967–) and Liam (1972–) Gallagher	Singers/musicians
4	Thomas Arthur, Baron de Tollendal (1702–66)	French military commander
5	Denis Leary (1957–)	Actor/comedian
6	John Lydon (Johnny Rotten) (1956–)	Singer/songwriter
7	Charles O'Brien (1699–1761)	Marshal of France
8	George O'Dowd (Boy George) (1961–)	Singer/songwriter
9	Bernardo O'Higgins (1778–1842)	President of Chile
10	Eugene O'Neill (1888–1953)	Writer

10

PEOPLE WITH AN IRISH MOTHER

	Name/Dates	What known for
1	Tony Blair (1953–)	Former British prime minister
2	Kate Bush (1958–)	Singer/songwriter
3	Raymond Chandler (1888–1959)	Writer
4	Henrique Couceiro (1861–1944)	Conqueror of Mozambique and governor of Angola
5	Amelia Edwards (1831–92)	Egyptologist
6	Greer Garson (1904–96)	Actress
7	Mel Gibson (1956–)	Actor/director
8	Paul McCartney (1942–)	Singer/songwriter/musician
9	Brian Mulroney (1939–)	18th prime minister of Canada
10	Louis St Laurent (1882–1973)	12th prime minister of Canada

PEOPLE WITH AN
IRISH GRANDFATHER

	Name/Dates	What known for
1	Mariah Carey (1970–)	Singer/songwriter
2	Richard J. Daley (1902–76)	Mayor of Chicago
3	Harrison Ford (1942–)	Actor
4	Grace Kelly (1929–82)	Actress
5	Joseph Kennedy (1888–1969)	Businessman/politician
6	Patricio Lynch (1825–86)	Chilean revolutionary
7	Patrice de MacMahon (1808–93)	Marshal of France
8	Natalie Merchant (1963–)	Singer
9	Eddie Murphy (1961–)	Actor/comedian
10	Edelmiro Farrell Plaul (1887–1980)	President of Argentina

10 PEOPLE WITH AN IRISH GRANDMOTHER

Name/Dates	What known for
1 Christina Aguilera (1980–)	Singer
2 Anne Boleyn (1507–36)	Queen of England
3 Joan Crawford (1905–77)	Actress
4 Ernesto Che Guevara (1928–67)	Argentino-Cuban revolutionary
5 Robert de Niro (1943–)	Actor
6 Alfredo di Stefano (1926–)	Footballer
7 Judy Garland (1922–69)	Actress
8 Mark McNulty (1953–)	Golfer
9 Winston Churchill (1874–1965)	British prime minister
10 Álvaro Obregón Salido (1880–1928)	Mexican president

WEALTHIEST PEOPLE*

	Name	Industry	Worth (€)
1	Pallonji Mistry	Industry	4.44 bn
2	John P. Grayken	Finance	3.98 bn
3	Hilary Weston	Retail	3.67 bn
4	Denis O'Brien	Telecoms/media	2.55 bn
5	John Dorrance	Investment	1.6 bn
6	Dermot Desmond	Investment	1.45 bn
7	Ellis Short	Finance	1.28 bn
8	Eamonn Cleary	Agribusiness	1.02 bn
9	Tony O'Reilly	News/media	1 bn
10	Sean Quinn	Insurance/industry	845 m

* Source: *Sunday Independent* Rich List, March 2010

WEALTHIEST PEOPLE IN 2001

	Name(s)	Industry	Worth (IR£)
1	John Dorrance	Inheritance	63 bn
2=	Tony O'Reilly	Media	61 bn
=	Chryss Goulandris	Food	61 bn
4	Tony Ryan	Airline	665 m
5	Dermot Desmond	Finance	576 m
6	U2	Pop music	475 m
7	Dr Allen McClay	Pharmaceuticals	472 m
8	Sean Quinn	Quarries/hotels/insurance/industry	352 m
9	Martin Naughton	Industry	339 m
10	Dennis O'Brien	Telecommunications	323 m

THE HISTORIC ISLE

DOGS

1 Bran and Sceolaing
These were the legendary hunting dogs of Fionn MacCumhaill (*c.*3rd century), commander in chief of the Fianna. Whenever the Fianna were hungry Bran, who stood the height of Fionn's shoulder, would go into the forest and take their meal to them.

2 Master McGrath
This greyhound won the Waterloo Cup (coursing event) in 1868, 1869 and 1871, was the subject of a famous ballad and has a statue in Clonmel. When he died his heart was found to be twice the size of a normal dog's heart.

3 Mick the Miller
Mick the Miller was the first greyhound to win the English Derby in successive years, 1929 and 1930. He lost in a re-run in 1931. He set nine world track records and starred in a film, *Wild Boy*, in 1935. After his death he was stuffed and he stood for many years in the Natural History Museum in London.

4 Patricia's Hope
From Ballymore Eustace, Co. Kildare, this greyhound achieved the Triple Crown (winning the English, Scottish and Welsh Derbies) in 1972 and was the second dog ever to win the English Derby in successive years, 1972 and 1973.

5 Shannon
Eamon de Valera presented this Irish cocker spaniel to John F. Kennedy in 1963.

6 Tinko
This was the beloved Pekinese dog of Hugh Lane (1875–1915), founder of the Dublin City Gallery.

7 Joseph Barcroft's dog
The Newry physiologist (1872–1947) exposed himself and the dog to hydrocyanic acid during the First World War to show how different species responded to toxic gases.

8 Samuel Haughton's dog
Haughton (1821–97) used to take his dog with him on his geology field trips.

9 Charles Barry's red setter
Barry (1823–97), a judge from Limerick, allowed the dog to follow him to court. Barry used to call for him at four o'clock and took the dog with him to his club.

10 White Bear
This dog belonged to the Archbishop of Dublin, Richard Whately (1787–1863). The dog learned to climb trees and used to jump into the water.

10 HIGH KINGS

1   **458–463 Lóeguire mac Néill**
The first king to convert to Christianity.

2   **544–565 Diarmait mac Cerbaill**
He was the last high king associated with Tara.

3   **797–817 Áed Oirdnide**
Áed Oirdnide was the first European king to be ordained (at Armagh), starting a tradition
that was adapted by most western European monarchies.

4   **846–860 Máel Sechnaill I**
The first to establish rule over all of Munster, he took hostages in 858.

5   **879–916 Flann Sinna**
The most famous of the Connacht-based kings, he was associated with Clonmacnoise.

6   **956–980 Domnall ua Néill**
Dómnall ua Néill was the first king to garrison subject sub-kingdoms. He based himself in
Míde and Brega leaving a kinsman to rule in Aileach.

7   **980–1002 Máel Sechnaill mac Domnaill**
King of Meath, he deposed Domnall in 980 and captured Dublin on three occasions before
submitting to Brían Bóruma in 1002. When Brian was killed at Clontarf he reassumed the
high kingship between 1014 and 1022.

8   **1002–14 Brían Bóruma**
The first high king from Munster, he defeated a revolt by Leinstermen and Dubliners in 999
and became sole king in 1002. He autographed the *Book of Armagh* as 'Emperor of the
Irish' in 1005, and had subdued the country by 1011. His forces won the Battle of Clontarf
against Leinster, Dublin, Manx and Orkney Island forces in 1014, but his battlefield death
plunged the country into a bitter 150-year contest for the kingship.

9   **1086–1119 Muirchertach Ua Bríain**
Bóruma's great grandson, he was a reformer who promoted the synods of Cashel and Ráith
Bressail in 1101 and 1111.

10 **1166–86 Rúaidrí Ua Conchóbair**
The last high king first claimed the kingship in 1156 and established his authority by 1166.
He died in 1198.

THINGS THAT HAPPENED IN 1916 APART FROM THE RISING

1   *Portrait of the Artist as a Young Man* by James Joyce was published.

2   A ban was placed on the taking of photographs at Irish race meetings.

3   Jim Kiernan's All Sorts won the Irish Grand National.

4   Tipperary came back from five points down to win the All-Ireland hurling final.

5   Mayo reached their first All-Ireland Gaelic football final, where they lost to Wexford.

6   *Henry V* was performed in Dublin to celebrate Shakespeare's 300th anniversary.

7   *Songs of the Fields* by Francis Ledwidge was published.

8   City of Dublin Steam Packet Company went on strike.

9   An entertainment tax was placed on cinemas, racecourses and sporting fixtures.

10 The main hall of the Dublin GPO was opened to the public for the first time.

SIEGES

1 1580 Smerwick
After they surrendered, 600 Spanish and Italian soldiers were massacred by English commander, Arthur Grey.

2 1645 Duncannon
The first conflict in Ireland in which mortars were employed. The Irish besieged and successfully took Duncannon from its English parliamentarian garrison.

3 1649 Drogheda
A Royalist, largely English, garrison under Arthur Aston defended for three days then surrendered. Official figures were that 3,500 were slain by Cromwell's men.

4 1649 Wexford
The city fell quickly. Cromwell's New Model Army ran amok, killing 2,000 in the market-place after an outpost had surrendered while peace talks were still in progress.

5 1649–50 Waterford
The first siege of the city was abandoned by Oliver Cromwell in 1649. In 1650 an outbreak of Bubonic plague caused the death of about 3,000 on each side.

6 1650 Clonmel
Cromwell's heaviest casualties on any battlefield, his soldiers burst through a false breach and were trapped in a killing ground prepared by Hugh Dubh O'Neill.

7 1651–2 Galway
The last city to surrender to Cromwell, the Irish commander Thomas Preston eventually had to give way due to food shortages and an outbreak of Bubonic plague.

8 1690 Derry
This 105-day siege, after apprentice boys had closed the city gates, during the Williamite War came to symbolize Protestant resistance to the armies of James II.

9 1690 Limerick
The third of four sieges in Limerick history was lifted when Patrick Sarsfield launched a daring raid behind Williamite lines to destroy enemy siege equipment at Ballyneety.

10 1961 Jadotville
The only siege involving serving Irish soldiers in the modern era, Pat Quinlan and his undersupplied Irish United Nations force held out for five days in the Congo.

MOST COSTLY CONFLICTS

	Dates	Conflict	Number of deaths
1	1641–60	Confederate and Cromwellian Wars	c.40,000 (plus an estimated 200,000 civilians)
2=	1688–91	Williamite Wars	c.30,000
=	1798	Rebellion	c.30,000
=	1914–18	First World War	c.30,000
5	1861–5	American Civil War	c.20,000
6	1939–45	Second World War	c.10.000 Irish
7	1969–98	Northern Ireland troubles	3,468
8	1919–21	War of Independence	c.1,400
9	1922–4	Civil War	c.2,000
10	1916	Rebellion	459

FAMOUS PEOPLE (9 MILITARY AND 1 BISHOP) WHO CHANGED SIDES

1 **Tom Barry (1897–1980)**
   This former British soldier later became a War of Independence hero of the Kilmichael Ambush.

2 **Roger Boyle (1621–79)**
   Boyle fought Murrough O'Brien in Cork (after O'Brien changed sides), then changed sides to Cromwell himself (the alternative was the Tower of London). He switched again to support Charles II in 1659.

3 **Lord Edward FitzGerald (1763–98)**
   Wounded and left for dead fighting with the British against the American rebels in South Carolina in 1871, he was one of the leaders of the 1798 Rebellion.

4 **Charles Coote (*c.*1610–61)**
   Coote started out a Royalist, switched to Parliament in the Confederate Wars and fought his old colleagues and the anti-Cromwell Scots. Against the Scots, he was saved by the Irish under Eoghan Rua O'Neill for reasons that are unclear. Had he changed sides again? He then went back to Cromwell and, eventually, in 1660 to the Royalists, just in time for the arrival of Charles II's regime.

5 **Máel Mórda (d. 1014)**
   The King of Leinster, based in Naas, he fought with the Vikings at Glenn Mama (999) and Clontarf (1014) against Brían Bóruma.

6 **W. R. E. Murphy (1890–1975)**
   From Wexford, Murphy was the youngest colonel in the British Army history when he attained the rank in 1915. He was a commanding officer of a British regiment in the First World War. He later joined the IRA. He became the first Irish commissioner of the Dublin Metropolitan Police and second in overall command of the National Army for a period in 1923.

7   **Murrough O'Brien (1614–74)**
The first Earl of Inchiquin, he converted to Protestantism and fought three major battles for the Royalists. He then switched to Cromwell's side to defeat former colleagues at Knocknanuss near Mallow in 1647. He converted back to the Catholic side while in exile in France in 1657, then returned to Ireland in 1663 as a supporter of Charles II.

8   **Eric Dorman O'Gowan (1895–1969)**
From Cootehill, he was the inspiration for Ernest Hemingway's 'Colonel Cantwell'. He was responsible for the mechanization of the British Army in the 1920s as Lieutenant General Eric Dorman-Smith and was a hero of the first Battle of El Alamein during the Second World War. He changed his name in 1949 and became a military adviser to the IRA.

9   **Robert Phaire (1619–82)**
A lieutenant colonel who switched to Cromwell in a negotiated exchange in 1648 and participated in the execution of Charles I.

10   **And a Bishop – Miler McGrath (1523–1622)**
He was the Catholic Bishop of Down and Connor, and Protestant Archbishop of Cashel at the same time, for a period of nine years. In all he held four bishoprics and 70 spiritualities and lived to be 100 in an era of turbulent religious wars.

10 GREAT BATTLES

1 **1014 Clontarf**
Brían Bóruma's Munster and Galwaymen faced Máel Mórda of Leinster, Sitric of Dublin, Sigurd from the Orkneys and Brodar from the Isle of Man on a site east of the Tolka. Brían's forces won, led by his son Murchad, but Brían's death destabilized the high kingship.

2 **1171 Dublin**
The Normans defeated Haskulf of Dublin twice in eight months. Their 200 knights, 400 other horsemen and 1,500 archers then crossed the bridge and routed the Irish high king's army at Castleknock, allegedly catching the king himself in his bath.

3 **1504 Knockdoe**
Garret Óg FitzGerald and his army of 6,000 defeated his son-in-law, Ulick de Burgh with 4,000 men, in the first Irish battle in which firearms were used.

4 **1598 The Yellow Ford**
Hugh O'Donnell and Hugh Maguire attacked Henry Bagenal's crown forces on the march with his 4,000 men and wiped out half his army.

5 **1601 Kinsale**
Aguila and 3,500 Spaniards arrived at Kinsale and were besieged by Charles Mountjoy and 6,900 men, while Hugh O'Neill, with 5,000 foot soldiers and 400 horsemen, marched the length of the country. The Irish withdrew to improve their position and then deployed before their main force had arrived. Aguila took no part in the battle and surrendered to Mountjoy nine days later.

6 **1646 Benburb**
Owen Roe O'Neill's army of 6,000 forced Robert Munro's army of the same strength back to the Blackwater River and wiped out half of Munro's force.

7 **1649 Rathmines**
After taking seven hours to march one mile, James Butler fell asleep. He awoke to find his army defeated, without having deployed the main body of his forces. Michael Jones had secured Dublin for the arrival of Oliver Cromwell.

8   1690 The Boyne

William of Orange's 36,000 Dutch, Huguenots, German, Danish, English, Enniskillen and Derry regiments defeated James II's 25,000 English, French, Irish, Dutch, Walloons and Germans. After a half-hour engagement, a third of William's army crossed the Boyne at Rosnaree. James overestimated the threat, was attacked as he retreated and fled to France. Losses were light, about 1,000 Jacobites and 500 Williamites.

9   1691 Aughrim

Two armies of 20,000 faced each other across a marsh. The Jacobites came close to capturing the Williamite guns before the Marquis de Saint Ruth, who had arrived from France two months earlier, was killed by a cannonball. The Jacobites lost 8,000 in a disorganized retreat.

10   1798 Arklow

Undersupplied insurgents defeated the Yeomen at Tubberneering, but when they reached Arklow it was barricaded by Francis Needham with 1,500 men. Casualties were low: 100 troops and 500 rebels, but hopes of a successful rebellion were ended.

10
MILITARY COMMANDERS

1 **Harold Alexander (b. London; 1891–1969)**
Raised in Caledon, Co. Tyrone, Alexander fought against Rommel in North Africa, commanded Allied forces in Italy in 1943 and became a field marshal in 1944.

2 **Herbert Kitchener (b. Ballylongford, Co. Kerry; 1850–1916)**
British secretary of state for war during the First World War, his face was famously used on army recruitment posters.

3 **Peter Lacy (b. Killeedy, Co. Limerick; 1678–1751)**
Lacy left for France at the age of 13 in 1691 to fight with the Irish Brigade. When his Athlone regiment was disbanded he fought for Austria, then Poland, then Russia. He gained credit for transforming the Russian Army into one of the best in Europe.

4 **Bernard Montgomery (b. London; 1887–1976)**
Raised in Moville, Co. Donegal, he was the first British general to win a major offensive against the Germans in the Second World War.

5 **Lavall Nugent (b. Ballinacor, Co. Wicklow; 1777–1862)**
Nugent became a field marshal in the Austrian Army.

6 **Charles O'Brien (b. Carrigaholt, Co. Clare; 1670–1706)**
His regiment distinguished itself at Blenheim, and Ramillies, where it captured a colour that was presented to a convent of Irish nuns at Ypres and is now in Kilmore Abbey in Galway.

7 **Daniel O'Mahoney (b. Cork; 1672–1714)**
O'Mahoney commanded Dillon's Regiment for France in a dramatic night-time attack on Cremona in 1702.

8 **Alejandro O'Reilly (b. Oldcastle, Co. Meath; 1722–94)**
He took Louisiana from the French colonists in 1768, remodelled the Spanish Army on Prussian lines and rose to the rank of field marshal.

9 **Patrick Sarsfield (b. Lucan, Co. Dublin; 1660–93)**
Commander of the 12,000 soldiers who went to France after the Treaty of Limerick, he fought at Steenkirk in 1692 and Landen in 1693, where he was mortally wounded.

10 **Arthur Wellesley (b. Dublin; 1769–1852)**
Wellesley was the commander of British forces, which, allied with the Prussian Army, defeated Napoleon at the Battle of Waterloo in 1815. He became Duke of Wellington.

THE 10
WORST DISASTERS

1 **1,198 dead**
The RMS *Lusitania* was torpedoed off the Old Head of Kinsale on 7 May 1915.

2 **501 dead**
On 10 October 1918 the RMS *Leinster* was torpedoed east of the Kish Bank.

3 **133 dead**
The MV *Princess Victoria* sank off Belfast on 31 January 1953.

4 **78 dead**
On 12 June 1889, a train filled with passengers on the Armagh Methodist Church Sunday School excursion stalled on a steep incline. The decision was taken to divide the train – the engine was to take four carriages to another station and then come back for the remaining eight. Stones were put under the rear carriage but as the train was split the rear carriages rolled backwards, down the incline and collided with another train.

5 **61 dead**
Aer Lingus Flight 712 disappeared on 24 March 1968. It was believed to have been shot down by an experimental missile.

6 **50 dead**
The French oil tanker *Betelgeuse* exploded on 8 January 1979 at the Whiddy oil terminal.

7= **48 dead**
On 5 September 1926 a timber barn in Dromcolliher being used as a temporary cinema caught fire.

= **48 dead**
The fire in the Stardust nightclub in Dublin on 14 February 1981 was believed to have started by someone setting light to a seat. Two hundred people were also injured.

9 **33 dead**
The SS *Irish Pine* was torpedoed on 15 November 1942.

10 **22 dead**
A moving train and a train waiting at a signal collided at Ballymacarrett Junction, Belfast, on a foggy morning on 10 January 1945.

The largest air disaster in Irish air space was on 23 June 1985 when Air India Flight 182 was destroyed by a bomb over the Atlantic, near Cork. This resulted in the loss of 329 lives.

MASTER MARINERS

1   Thomas Andrews (b. Comber, Co. Down; 1873–1912)
This Belfast shipbuilder became known as 'The Admiral'.

2   John Barry (b. Tacumshane, Co. Wexford; 1745–1803)
Barry was credited as 'The Father of the American Navy'.

3   Charles Beresford (b. Dundalk; 1846–1919)
He became an admiral and was one of the best-known British sailors of his day.

4   William Brown (b. Foxford, Co. Mayo; 1777–1857)
Brown was known as 'The Father of the Argentinian Navy'.

5   Andrew Cunningham (b. Rathmines, Dublin; 1883–1963)
Cunningham served as commander-in-chief of the Mediterranean Fleet in the Second World War. In 1943 he was promoted to first sea lord.

6   John de Robeck (b. Naas, Co. Kildare; 1862–1928)
An admiral in the British Royal Navy, he commanded naval forces in the Dardanelles during the Second World War.

7   Robert Halpin (b. Tinakilly, Co. Wicklow; 1836–94)
Halpin was the captain of the SS *Great Eastern*, which laid ocean telegraph cables in the 1860s and 1870s.

8   Charles Nugent (1759–1844)
This British admiral distinguished himself in battles against the Spanish in Honduras.

9   Daniel O'Honyn (b. Ennistymon; *c.*1710–73)
O'Honyn was an admiral in the Spanish Navy who became governor of Ferrol. The chalice he presented to the parish of Killaspuglonane is still in use.

10   Richard Roberts (b. Ardmore, Passage West, Co. Cork; 1803–41)
He captained the *Sirius* when it became the first steam-powered vessel to cross the Atlantic in 1838.

SHIPWRECKS

1   **14 September 1588** *La Trinidad Valencera*
    This warship of the Spanish Armada was wrecked in a storm in Kinnegoe Bay off Innishowen. Over the years divers recovered bronze cannons, weapons, stringed instruments, wheels, navigational tools, grenades and pottery.

2   **27 October 1588 SV** *Girona*
    Off Lacada Point near Dunluce, Co. Antrim, this galleass sunk in a storm. Diving is prohibited within a certain area around the wreck site although the wreck itself no longer remains. Its treasure is now on display in the Ulster Museum, Belfast.

3   **14 October 1914 HMS** *Audacious*
    This 23,000-ton battleship was mined in Lough Swilly.

4   **13 April 1917 SS** *Bandon*
    An armed steamer, it was torpedoed off Minehead, Co. Waterford.

5   **2 October 1917 HMS** *Drake*
    This armoured cruiser was torpedoed off Ballycastle. The remains of the wreck were blown up in 1979.

6   **4 March 1918 SS** *Castle Eden*
    Torpedoed off Innistrahull, Co. Donegal, ammunition from her defensive gun is still lying around.

7   **4 March 1947 MV** *Bolivar*
    This Norwegian motor vessel ran aground in a snowstorm off Kish Bank.

8   **1 August 1986 MV** *Contessa VIV*
    A Spanish factory ship, it struck rocks off Ardnakilla Point, Castletownbere.

9   **22 November 1986 MV** *Kowloon Bridge*
    This 274-m (900-ft) long super bulk carrier ran aground in a gale off Toe Head, Baltimore, Co. Cork. It is the largest wreck by tonnage in the world.

10 **25 December 2000 MFV** *Zorro Zaurre*
    A Spanish trawler, the wreckage is located off Castletownbere, Co. Cork.

There are 10,243 shipwrecks off the Irish coast according to the Irish Underwater Council.

10 HIGHWAYMEN

1 **Willie Brennan (d. 1804)**
Brennan on the Moor, from Fermoy, who said, 'I own that I did rob the rich and did the poor supply.'

2 **Dudley Costello (d. 1667)**
This former Spanish colonel commanded a force of 200 men and burned a castle in Mayo.

3 **William Crotty (d. 1742)**
Comeragh highwayman who became the subject of a famous lament, supposedly written by his wife.

4 **Charles Dempsey (d. 1735)**
Dempsey was a horse thief from Laois, hence his nickname, Cathaoir na gCapall, 'Charles of the Horses'.

5 **James Freney (d. 1788)**
Established as a figure in popular mythology through his biography, after he turned informer on his colleagues in April 1749 and became a customs official at New Ross.

6 **Captain Gallagher (d. 1818)**
From Ballina, he once forced a landlord to eat his eviction notices.

7 **Redmond O'Hanlon (1620–81)**
O'Hanlon was murdered in his sleep by his foster brother at Hilltown, Co. Down, for a £200 reward.

8 **Naoise O'Haughan (1691–1720)**
This Antrim highwayman's headquarters were on the Black Mountain above Belfast.

9 **Edmund O'Ryan (1670–1724)**
Immortalized in the song 'Éamonn an Chnoic', 'Ned of the Hill'. He led a band of rapparees after his land was confiscated.

10 **Captain Richard Power**
From Cork, Power was known as the 'Genteel Robber'. On one occasion he robbed the father of a bride and then toasted the bride before making his getaway.

PLACES WHERE PUBLIC EXECUTIONS TOOK PLACE

1 Market Square, Clonmel

2 Gallows Green, Limerick

3 Gallows Hill, Kilkenny

4 George's Hill, Dublin

5 Harold's Cross Green, Dublin

6 Kilmainham Common, Dublin

7 Knockcroghery, Roscommon

8 St Stephen's Green, Dublin

9 In front of St Catherine's Church, Thomas Street, Dublin

10 Wexford Bridge

10
EXECUTION MILESTONES

1   **1353 Last public burning for heresy**
    Two members of the MacNamara family in Clare on orders of the Bishop of Waterford.

2   **1766 Last martyrdom**
    Fr Nicholas Sheehy at Clonmel.

3   **1798 Last to be hanged, drawn and quartered**
    William and Henry Sheares in Dublin.

4   **1803 Last beheading**
    Robert Emmet was hanged and decapitated on Thomas Street Dublin.

5   **1830 Last man hanged for forgery**
    Peter Comyn in Ennis, Co. Clare.

6   **1835 Last man hanged for rape**
    Michael Quinlan in Limerick.

7   **1866 Last public hanging**
    John Logue, Downpatrick. Newspapers reported there were about 300 people present.

8   **1870 First private hanging**
    Andrew Carr in Richmond Prison on the South Circular Road, Dublin.

9   **1925 Last woman hanged for murder**
    Annie Walsh, Mountjoy Prison, Dublin.

10 **1961 Last man hanged for murder**
    Robert McGladdery from Newry, in Crumlin Road Gaol, Belfast. The last in the Republic
    was Michael Manning, hanged at Mountjoy Prison, Dublin, in 1954.

    In 1848, Thomas Francis Meagher became the last person to be sentenced to be hanged,
    drawn (disembowelled) and quartered (beheaded and cut into four parts). However,
    his sentence was commuted to transportation and he went on to become MP for
    Waterford and governor of Montana, USA.

    The death penalty was abolished in law in 1990, and has been specifically prohibited by
    the Constitution of Ireland since 2002.

EVENTS THAT OCCURRED ON FRIDAY 13TH

1   **Friday 13 March 1592**
    The foundation stone of the College of the Holy and Undivided Trinity (Trinity College, University of Dublin) was laid by the mayor, Thomas Smith, on the site of the former priory of All Hallows.

2   **Friday 13 July 1635**
    Co. Mayo passed to English rule.

3   **Friday 13 September 1723**
    The Wood's halfpence came into circulation.

4   **Friday 13 April 1742**
    Frederick Handel's *Messiah* was performed for the first time. It was sung by the choirs of St Patrick's and Christ Church, Dublin, at the New Music Hall in Fishamble Street. Proceeds of £400 went to the relief of prisoners, Mercer's Hospital and the Charitable Infirmary.

5   **Friday 13 September 1844**
    Daniel O'Connell and the repeal leaders were released after their trial and sentence for conspiracy was overturned.

6   **Friday 13 November 1863**
    Decision was made to open St Stephen's Green in Dublin to the public. Due to a series of delays by Dublin Corporation and at Westminster, it took 17 years for the decision to be approved.

7   **Friday 13 April 1906**
    Samuel Beckett was born in Cooldrinagh, Dublin.

8   **Friday 13 September 1907**
    The central fire station in Tara Street, Dublin opened.

9   **Friday 13 April 1928**
    A Bremen monoplane, crewed by Colonel James Fitzmaurice, Captain Hermann Kohl and Baron Gunther von Hunefeld, flew from Baldonnell Airport, Co. Dublin to Greenly Island, Labrador, Canada. It was the first east–west transatlantic flight. The aircraft averaged a speed of 95 kph (59 mph) throughout the 30-hour journey.

10 **Friday 13 September 1968**
    The first Merriman School opened in Ennis, Co. Clare.

10 UNUSUAL BURIAL PLACES OF HISTORICAL FIGURES

	Name	What known for	Where buried
1	Dion Boucicault (1820–90)	Writer	Mount Hope Cemetery, Rochester, USA
2	St Brendan (c.484–577)	Early Irish monastic saint	Clonfert, Co. Galway
3	Robert Emmet (1778–1803)	Revolutionary	Unknown
4	Arthur Guinness (1725–1803)	Brewer	Oughter Ard, Co. Kildare
5	Jack Kelly (1862–95)	Boxer	Mount Calvary Cemetery, Oregon, USA
6	John Mitchel (1815–75)	Patriot	Drumcree, Co. Armagh
7	Turlough O'Carolan (1670–1738)	Harper	Keadue, Co. Roscommon
8	Hugh Roe O'Donnell (1572–1602)	Military leader	Franciscan monastery Valladolid, Spain
9	Hugh O'Neill (c.1550–1616)	Military leader	San Pietro in Montorio, Rome
10	Oscar Wilde (1854–1900)	Writer	Père Lachaise Cemetery, Paris, France

Oscar Wilde was originally buried in the Cimetière de Bagneux outside Paris but was later moved to Père Lachaise Cemetery in the city.

GODS FROM CELTIC MYTHOLOGY

1 **Aonghus**
He was a chieftain of the Tuatha dé Danaan, who resided at Newgrange.

2 **Balar**
A fearsome warrior with a destructive eye, slain by Lugh at Moytura.

3 **Crom Dubh**
A dark god whose statue in Cavan was demolished by St Patrick.

4 **Daghda**
Daghda was the principal deity of Tuatha dé Danaan.

5 **Daire**
Believed to be the fruitful one, a great ancestor for several Irish septs.

6 **Donn**
One reference describes him as 'the king of the dead, at the red tower of the dead.' He is also referred to as the 'Dark One'.

7 **Goibhniu**
This deity was the god of smiths and is recorded as being a leading artisan of the Tuatha dé Danaan.

8 **Lugh**
The harvest god, referred to as the 'Shining One'.

9 **Nuadhu**
The hunter-god with water associations. He is believed to have brought the Lia Fáil stone to Ireland.

10 **Oghma**
He was the god of learning.

10 GODDESSES FROM CELTIC MYTHOLOGY

1 **Aine**
She was the goddess of Munster, sovereignty and agricultural prosperity.

2 **Aoibheall**
Known as the 'Lovely One', she was the protectress of the Dál g Cais (a great clan of northern Munster).

3 **Banba**
The goddess of the spirit of Ireland, she had two sisters, Ériu and Fódhla. On arrival in Ireland, all of the sisters asked for the island to be named after them. Ériu was given the honour, although Banba's name was sometimes used.

4 **Boinn**
Boinn was the goddess of the Boyne, the most important of the Irish rivers.

5 **Brigid**
Poetess, and the goddess of crafts, agricultural fertility, and domestic animals, St Brigid of Kildare assumed some of her special characteristics.

6 **Danu**
Mother-goddess and food-provider, the Tuatha dé Danaan were named after her.

7 **Éadaoin or Étaín**
She may have originally been a sun-goddess. She is most associated with the story *Tochmarc Étaine*, of which she is the heroine.

8 **Macha**
The land-goddess of Ulster, the county of Armagh takes it's name from her. It was originally called 'Ard Macha', meaning 'Macha heights'.

9 **Medb**
She was the goddess of Connacht and female sexuality.

10 **Mor-Rioghain**
Related to Macha through Nuadh, she was the goddess of land and war.

SAINTS OF EARLY IRELAND

1 **Adomnán (625–704) Feast day: 23 September**
Donegal-born abbot of Iona in 687, he drew up laws protecting civilians in times of war.

2 **Aengus (d. 824) Feast day: 11 March**
Born in Clonengh, he was the leader of the Ceile De monastic reform movement.

3 **Ailbe (d. 528) Feast day: 12 September**
Ailbe was the founder of Emly, Co. Tipperary, and patron of wolves.

4 **Brendan (*c.*484–577) Feast day: 16 May**
Born near Tralee, he founded monasteries at Clonfert. The story of his voyages included a reputed journey to America, which was a medieval 'bestseller'.

5 **Brigid (d. 525) Feast day: 1 February**
The founder of Kildare, Brigid was born in Faughart. She was the subject of the first great Irish hagiographical work.

6 **Ciarán (*c.*516–546) Feast day: 9 September**
He was the founder of one of the most important early monasteries, Clonmacnoise, at the crossroads of the Shannon and the Eiscir Riata in the heart of Ireland.

7 **Columbanus (d. 615) Feast day: 24 November**
Commonly regarded as one of Ireland's greatest missionary saints and scholars. Examples of his writings of his extensive travels have survived.

8 **Columcille (521–97) Feast day: 9 June**
He was an advocate of monasticism and the founder of Iona.

9 **Gall (550–646) Feast day: 16 October**
Gall lived as a hermit in the forests south-west of Lake Constance and founded St Gallen in Switzerland.

10 **Kevin (d. 618) Feast day: 3 June**
He was the founder and first abbot of Glendalough, the chief pilgrimage destination in early Ireland.

RELIGIOUS FOUNDERS

1 **John Abernathy (1680–1740)**
Derry-born Abernathy disowned the church court system. His followers later became Unitarians.

2 **Mary Aikenhead (1787–1858)**
Born in Cork, she was the founder of the Irish Sisters of Charity in 1815 and the Our Lady's Hospice in 1845.

3 **John Nelson Darby (1800–82)**
Darby formed the Plymouth Brethren with John Cronin in a Dublin church in 1827.

4 **Thomas Kelly (1769–1855)**
His religion, the Kellyites, established ten congregations in Ireland in 1803.

5 **Catherine McAuley (1778–1841)**
Born near Santry, Dublin, she was the founder of the Sisters of Mercy in 1831 for the education of poor girls. McAuley was declared 'Venerable' in 1990.

6 **Francis Makemie (1658–1708)**
From Ramelton, Makemie was considered to be the founder of Presbyterianism in the USA.

7 **Mother Mary Martin (1892–1975)**
This Glenageary-born nurse founded the Medical Missionaries of Mary in 1937.

8 **Nano Nagle (1718–84)**
Born at Ballygriffin, near Mallow, Nagle was the founder of the Presentation Sisters.

9 **Edmund Ignatius Rice (1762–1844)**
Rice was born in Callan and was the founder of the Irish Christian Brothers and Presentation Brothers orders. He was beatified in 1996.

10 **John Walker (1768–1833)**
From Roscommon town, he founded the 'Church of God', or Walkerite Church, at Stafford Street in Dublin in 1803.

RELIGIOUS CONTROVERSIES

1   Pelagianism
    This was the fifth-century controversy that caused the Pope to send Palladius as the first
    Bishop of the Irish in the 430s.

2   Copyright
    St Columcille's refusal to hand over a copy of St Finian's psalms that he had made in secret
    led to King Diarmuid's ruling: 'To every cow its calf and to every book its copy.' This is
    regarded as the first copyright judgment.

3   Easter
    The St Jerome calculation of Easter was kept by the Celtic Church in opposition to the
    Roman calculation, even after the Synod of Whitby in 664.

4   Virgin Mary
    In 1328 Adam Dubh Ó Túatháil was burned for heresy at what is now College Green,
    Dublin, for denying the sanctity of the Virgin Mary.

5   Dunboyne controversy
    John Butler (1731–1800) resigned the Catholic bishopric of Cork in 1786, became a
    Protestant to inherit the title of Baron Dunboyne and married to produce an heir.

6   Second Reformation
    A heated evangelical campaign organized by fundamentalists in the Church of Ireland and
    Church of England in the 1820s.

7   Brethren
    Founded in the late 1820s in Dublin by Anthony Groves (1795–1853) and John Darby
    (1800–82), it later split into the 'Open' and 'Closed' Brethren.

8   Arianism
    A middle ground between Calvinism and Presbyterianism, a campaign by Henry Cooke
    (1788–1868) caused a split in 1830.

9   Birr Schism
    Father Michael Crotty and his cousin, Fr William Crotty, broke away from the Catholic
    Church to form their own church in Birr in the 1830s.

10 Elim
    George Jeffreys (1889–1962) founded the Elim Pentecostal Church in Monaghan in 1915,
    which was a breakaway from the Welsh Congregational Church.

10 PEOPLE WHO CHANGED RELIGION

1 **Thomas Barnardo (1845–1905)**
Founder of homes for destitute children, Barnardo converted from Catholicism during a Protestant religious revival in 1862.

2 **William Carleton (1794–1869)**
He had once hoped to become a Catholic priest, but he fell in love with a Protestant woman, Jane Anderson, and converted.

3 **Roger Casement (1864–1916)**
Casement became a Catholic days before he was hanged for treason in Pentonville Prison in August 1916.

4 **William Conolly (1662–1729)**
Speaker of the House of Commons, Conolly was born into a Catholic family in Donegal but converted for his 'personal enrichment'.

5 **Aubrey de Vere (1814–1902)**
A friend of Cardinal Newman, de Vere converted to Catholicism in 1851.

6 **Rex Ingram (1893–1950)**
The Hollywood film director converted to Islam.

7 **Maud Gonne MacBride (1866–1953)**
She was brought up a Protestant but became a Catholic shortly before she married Major John MacBride in 1903.

8 **Constance Markievicz (1868–1927)**
Markievicz became a Catholic after being sentenced to death for her part in the 1916 Easter Rising.

9 **George Augustus Moore (1852–1933)**
Brought up a Catholic, Moore converted to Protestantism late in life.

10 **Oscar Wilde (1854–1900)**
Wilde became a Catholic on the day that he died.

COUNTRIES AND THEIR IRISH DIASPORA

	Country	Irish diaspora
1	USA	34.7 million
2	Britain	6 million
3	Canada	4.3 million
4	Australia	1.9 million
5	Argentina	500,000
6=	France	200,000
=	Spain	200,000
8	Mexico	90,000
9	South Africa	50,000
10	New Zealand	40,000

Figures on the Irish diaspora community in the USA and Britain vary widely, 35–44 million people in the US and 5–14 million of British people have an Irish parent or grandparent, 10 per cent of the British population. We have used the figure from the British census, although the ethnic question was highly contentious. In June 2010 the Irish Government announced plans to introduce a certificate of Irish heritage for up to 70 million people of Irish descent around the world who do not qualify for citizenship.

PHILANTHROPISTS AND CAMPAIGNERS

1   **Theodosia Blachford (1745–1817)**
     A significant figure in Methodism, Blachford established the Female Orphan House in 1790 and the House of Refuge in 1802, both in Dublin.

2   **Richard Martin (b. Dublin; 1754–1834)**
     Co-founder of the Society of Prevention of Cruelty to Animals, he was nicknamed 'Humanity Dick'.

3   **Joseph Barrington (b. Cabinteely; 1764–1846)**
     The founder of the Fever Hospital and House of Recovery in Dublin's Cork Street.

4   **William Hickey (b. Cork; 1787–1875)**
     Hickey was an active campaigner for agricultural reform.

5   **Mary Letitia Martin (b. Ballynahinch Castle, Connemara; 1815–50)**
     Her devotion to the poor during the famine earned her the title of the Princess of Connemara.

6   **Sarah Atkinson (b. Athlone; 1823–93)**
     A reformer who founded the St Joseph's Industrial Institute and helped establish the Temple Street Children's Hospital in 1872.

7   **Arthur Guinness (b. Dublin; 1840–1915)**
     Arthur Edward Guinness was the great-grandson of the original Arthur Guinness, founder of the Guinness brewery. Like many other members of the Guinness family, Arthur Edward was a philanthropist and is most remembered for funding and creating St Stephen's Green in Dublin.

8   **Thomas John Barnardo (b. Dublin; 1845–1905)**
     Founder of Dr Barnardo's Homes in 1868, he wanted to 'rescue children from the streets'.

9   **James Larkin (b. Liverpool; 1876–1947)**
     The son of Irish parents, Larkin was the founder of the Irish trade union movement and campaigned for better conditions for workers.

10   **Hugh Lane (b. Cork; 1875–1915)**
     An art dealer, Lane donated his collection and founded the Municipal Gallery of Modern Art in Dublin in January 1908. Reputedly, this was the first public gallery of modern art in the world. The gallery is now called the Hugh Lane Gallery.

MEDICAL PIONEERS

1 **Abraham Colles (b. Millmount, Kilkenny; 1773–1843)**
Colles received his MD in 1797. He became the president of the Royal College of Surgeons and under his leadership the college became one of the most respected in Europe. A fracture of the wrist involving a break of the end of the radius bone of the forearm is called a 'Colles fracture'.

2 **Arthur Jacob (b. Portlaoise; 1790–1874)**
An ophthalmologist, he discovered the *Jacobi membrane* in the eye and described the condition 'Jacob's Ulcer'. He was a co-founder of the City of Dublin Hospital in 1832 and started the Dublin Medical Press.

3 **Robert James Graves (b. Dublin; 1796–1853)**
Graves was the first physician to describe exophthalmic goiter, subsequently named 'Grave's Disease'.

4 **Francis Rynd (b. Dublin; 1801–61)**
He was the inventor of the hypodermic needle and syringe.

5 **Dominic John Corrigan (b. Dublin; 1802–80)**
This physician was particularly remembered for his significant work during the Famine, and he established the connection between famine and fever.

6 **William Stokes (b. Dublin; 1804–78)**
Stokes was a pioneer of new methods of clinical diagnosis and wrote the first book in English about the use of the stethoscope.

7 **William Wilde (b. Castlerea, Co. Roscommon; 1815–76)**
The father of writer Oscar, William ran his own eye and ear hospital in Dublin. He was a pioneer in the use of atrophine.

8 **Arthur Leared (b. Wexford; 1822–79)**
Leared invented the double stethoscope.

9 **Edward Hallaran Bennett (b. Cork; 1837–1907)**
A president of the Royal College of Surgeons in Ireland, he invented the Bennett's double ring splint and described the Bennett's fracture in 1881.

10 **Vincent Barry (b. Cork; 1908–75)**
Regarded as one of Ireland's unsung heroes, he developed a treatment for leprosy in the 1950s.

10 ENGINEERS

1   Louis Brennan (b. Castlebar, Co. Mayo; 1852–1932)
    Invention: Dirigible torpedo and version of helicopter

2   Richard Edgeworth (b. Bath, raised Edgeworthstown, Co. Longford; 1744–1817)
    Invention: Road-building system

3   Harry Ferguson (b. Growell, Co. Down; 1884–1960)
    Invention: Standardized hydraulic lift for farm tractor

4   James Joseph Hicks (b. Rosscarbery, Co. Cork; 1837–1916)
    Invention: Clinical thermometer

5   Robert Mallet (b. Dublin; 1810–81)
    Invention: Father of modern seismology

6   Thomas McLoughlin (b. Drogheda, Co. Louth; 1896–1971)
    Invention: Shannon hydro-electric scheme

7   Alexander Mitchell (b. Dublin; 1780–1868)
    Invention: Screw-pile system for constructing lighthouses, fixing beacons and mooring ships

8   Charles Parsons (b. London; 1854–1931)
    Invention: Improved steam turbine for power stations and ships

9   James Ryan (b. Castlecomer; c.1770–1847)
    Invention: Trepanning cutter for mines and tunnels

10 John Walker (b. Castlecomer, Co. Kilkenny; 1841–1901)
    Invention: Caterpillar tracks for rough terrain

INVENTORS

10

1   **William Reid Clanny** (b. Bangor, Co. Down; 1776–1850)
Invention: Mining safety lamp

2   **Aeneas Coffey** (b. Dublin; *c.*1780–1852)
Invention: Heat exchanger and improved still

3   **Samuel Cleland Davidson** (b. Belfast; 1846–1921)
Invention: Tea-processing machinery

4   **John Boyd Dunlop** (b. Ayrshire; 1840–1921)
Invention: Pneumatic tyre

5   **John Holland** (b. Liscannor, Co. Clare; 1841–1914)
Invention: Modern submarine

6   **John Joly** (b. Clonbullogue, Co. Offaly; 1857–1933)
Invention: Radiotherapy and modern colour photography

7   **John Howard Kyan** (b. Dublin; 1774–1850)
Invention: 'Kyanization' timber preservative

8   **James Martin** (b. Crossgar, Co Down; 1893–1981)
Invention: Ejector seat

9   **James William McGauley** (b. Kilmainham, Dublin; *c.*1806–67)
Invention: Trembler interrupter for electric bells

10   **Richard Pockrich** (b. Aghnamallagh, Co. Monaghan; *c.*1696–1759)

Invention: Musical glass

10
MATHEMATICIANS

1   William Rowan Hamilton (b. Dublin; 1805–65)
Regarded as the father of linear algebra, he discovered the four quaternion components.

2   James McCullagh (b. Landahussy, Co. Tyrone; 1809–47)
This Trinity College lecturer developed the mathematical framework for optical phenomena.

3   George Boole (b. Lincoln; 1815–64)
Appointed as the first professor of mathematics of Queen's College, Cork, Boolean algebra formed the basis of modern computer arithmetic.

4   George Stokes (b. Skreen, Co. Sligo; 1819–1903)
A physicist and mathematician who developed Stokes Theorem and Stokes-Navier equations.

5   George Salmon (b. Cork; 1819–1904)
A pioneer in algebraic geometry.

6   John Casey (b. Kilkenny; 1820–91)
Casey was the co-developer of the geometry of the circle and the triangle.

7   George Francis FitzGerald (b. Dublin; 1851–1901)
His contraction theory presaged Einstein's theory of relativity.

8   Alicia Boole Stott (b. Cork; 1860–1940)
Stott was the first to describe polytopes in four dimensions.

9   William McFadden Orr (b. Comber, Co. Down; 1866–1934)
Orr developed the Orr-Sommerfeld equation with Arnold Sommerfeld.

10   John Lighton Synge (b. Dublin; 1897–1995)
He worked on developing Einstein's theory of relativity.

PHYSICISTS

10

1   John Stewart Bell (b. Belfast; 1928–90)
Work: Bell's Inequalities outlined the connections between physics and geometry

2   Susan Jocelyn Bell Burnell (b. Belfast; 1943–)
Work: Discovered the first pulsar

3   Lucien Bull (b. Dublin; 1876–1972)
Work: Improved electrocardiograph; pioneer of high-speed photography

4   Nicholas Callan (b. Darver, Co. Louth; 1799–1864)
Work: Induction coil, electric battery and principle of the dynamo

5   James Drumm (b. Co Down; 1896–1974)
Work: Developed the nickel-zinc rechargeable battery

6   Thomas Grubb (b. Waterford; 1800–78)
Work: Improved telescope refractor for photography

7   Joseph Larmor (b. Magheragall, Co. Antrim; 1857–1942)
Work: Showed how wireless electric rays bend around the earth

8   William Thomson, Baron Kelvin (b. Belfast; 1824–1907)
Work: Kelvin temperature scale

9   John Tyndall (b. Leighlinbridge, Co. Carlow; 1820–93)
Work: Forerunner of the fibre-optic cable and discontinuous heating for killing bacteria in milk (tyndallization)

10   Ernest Walton (b. Dungarvan, Co. Waterford; 1903–95)
Work: First to artificially split the atom with fellow student John Cockcroft in 1932; later awarded the Nobel Prize in Physics in 1951

10
BIOLOGISTS*

1 **George Allman (b. Cork; 1812–98)**
Work: The first to name the endoderm and ectoderm

2 **John Desmond Bernal (b. Nenagh, Co. Tipperary; 1901–71)**
Work: Major contributions to X-ray crystallography

3 **Patrick Browne (b. Claremorris, Co. Mayo; c.1720–90)**
Work: Named 104 genera

4 **Thomas Coulter (b. Dundalk, Co. Louth; 1793–1843)**
Work: Surveyed the wildlife of Mexico and Alta California

5 **Henry Dixon (b. Dublin; 1869–1953)**
Work: Proposed the 'tension' theory of sap ascent

6 **Ellen Hutchins (b. Bantry, Co. Cork; 1785–1815)**
Work: An authority on mosses, ferns, lichens and seaweeds

7 **John Macoun (b. Magheralin, Co. Down; 1831–1920)**
Work: Catalogued 100,000 Canadian flora and fauna

8 **Joseph Barclay Pentland (b. Armagh; 1797–1873)**
Work: surveyed the wildlife of the Bolivian Andes and inspired Darwin

9 **Robert Lloyd Praeger (b. Holywood, Co. Down; 1865–1953)**
Work: Author of the enormously influential *Irish Topographical Botany*

10 **Edward Sabine (b. Dublin; 1788–1883)**
Work: Surveyed the birds of Greenland; Sabine's Gull is named for him

* List includes biologists and botanists (botany being a branch of biology)

CHEMISTS

1 **Thomas Andrews (b. Belfast; 1813–85)**
Work: Showed that ozone is another form of oxygen

2 **James Apjohn (b. Pallasgreen, Co. Limerick; 1796–1886)**
Work: Discovered Apjohnite and Jellettite

3 **Francis Beaufort (b. Navan, Co. Meath; 1774–1857)**
Work: Developed a 13-point wind scale in 1805 (it now goes to 17)

4 **Robert Boyle (b. Lismore, Co. Waterford; 1627–91)**
Work: Father of modern chemistry; invented Boyle's Law

5 **Richard Chevenix (b. Dublin; 1774–1830)**
Work: Proved elemental nature of palladium

6 **William Higgins (b. Collooney, Co. Sligo; 1763–1825)**
Work: Early proponent of atomic theory

7 **Robert Kane (b. Dublin; 1809–90)**
Work: Proved the existence of the ethyl radical

8 **Richard Kirwan (b. Kinvara, Co. Galway; 1733–1812)**
Work: Developed first table of specific heats

9 **Kathleen Lonsdale (b. Newbridge, Co. Kildare; 1903–71)**
Work: Discovered the structure of benzene

10 **George Johnstone Stoney (b. Clareen, Co. Offaly; 1826–1911)**
Work: Invented the term 'electron' and predicted the existence of missing elements

10 EXPLORERS

1 **John Ball (b. Dublin; 1818–89)**
Ball has an Alpine pass, Passa di Ball, named after him. He was a pioneer in glacial theory.

2 **St Brendan (*c.*484–577)**
A sailor, his transatlantic adventures inspired Christopher Columbus.

3 **Robert O'Hara Burke (b. Craughwell, Co. Galway; 1820–61)**
He died of starvation as he crossed Australia from south to north with his companion William Wills in 1861.

4 **Tom Crean (b. Annascaul, Co. Kerry; 1877–1938)**
Crean went on three expeditions to Antarctica between 1911 and 1917.

5 **Francis Crozier (b. Banbridge, Co. Down; 1796–1848)**
Crozier took command of an ill-fated expedition to find the Northwest Passage after John Franklin's death in 1847, only to perish himself a month later.

6 **James of Ireland (*fl.* 1316–30)**
This 14th-century adventurer travelled to Sumatra and China.

7 **Francis McClintock (b. Dundalk, Co. Louth; 1819–1907)**
McClintock discovered the fate of John Franklin. A channel in northern Canada is named after him.

8 **Robert McClure (b. Wexford; 1807–73)**
He discovered the Northwest Passage in 1850.

9 **Mark Pollock (b. Holywood, Co. Down; 1976–)**
This adventurer was the first blind man to reach the South Pole.

10 **Ernest Shackleton (b. Kilkea, Co Kildare; 1874–1922)**
Shackleton conducted three separate expeditions to Antartica. In the disastrous third expedition of 1915 his ship, *Endurance*, was crushed by ice in the Weddell Sea. This resulted in an epic voyage of 1,287 km (800 miles) to reach safety in South Georgia in the *James Caird*, a 6.7-m (22-ft) lifeboat.

TRADE AND INDUSTRY

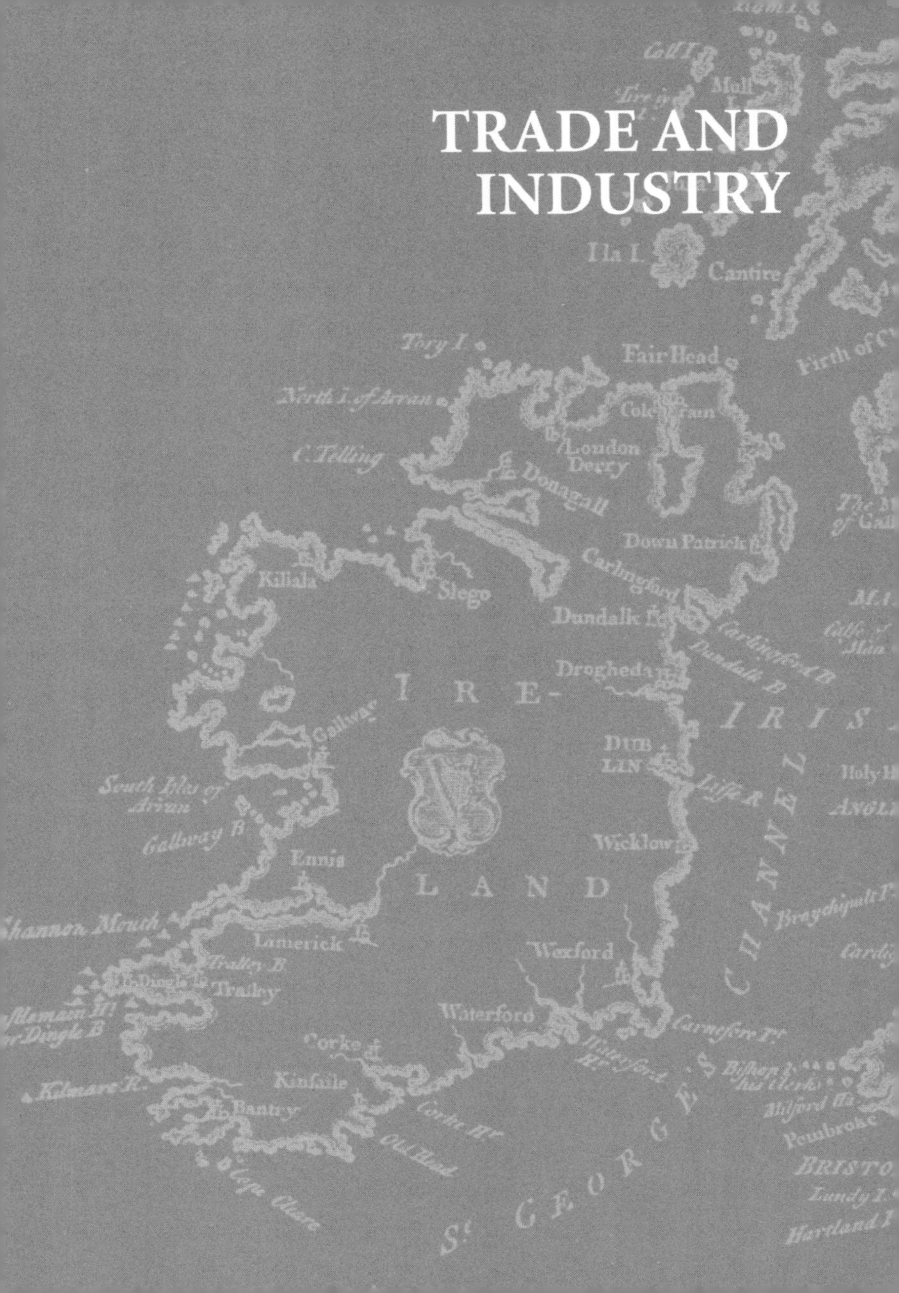

10 ARCHITECTS

1 **George Coppinger Ashlin (b. Little Island, Co. Cork; 1837–1921)**
Ashlin worked with Edward Pugin on Cobh Cathedral, which is seen by some as the realization of the ideal Gothic church.

2 **Nathaniel Clements (1705–77)**
A property developer, Clements influenced Irish architecture and may have designed Áras an Uachtaráin himself.

3 **James Gandon (b. London; 1743–1823)**
Having worked on significant building in England, Gandon arrived in Ireland in 1781. His signature buildings are the Four Courts and Custom House in Dublin.

4 **James Hoban (b. Callan, Co. Kilkenny; 1758–1831)**
Hogan is best known for designing the White House in Washington, D.C.

5   Thomas Ivory (b. Cork; 1732–86)
     This Cork-born architect designed the Incorporated Law Society building in Blackhall
     Place, Dublin.

6   James Joseph McCarthy (b. Dublin; 1817–82)
     An associate of Edward Pugin, McCarthy designed seven cathedrals and nearly
     50 churches during the 19th-century ecclesiastical building boom.

7   Liam McCormick (b. Derry; 1916–96)
     McCormick was the architect of iconic north-western churches such as those at Burt,
     Meelick, Gortahork and Steelstown.

8   Richard Morrison (b. Cork; 1767–1849)
     Designer of country houses, including: Baronscourt, Co. Tyrone; Killruddery, Co.
     Wicklow; Ballyfin, Co. Laois; and Fota, Co. Cork.

9   Edward Lovett Pearce (b. Co. Meath; 1699–1733)
     The father of Palladianism in Ireland, Lovett Pearce was the designer of the Irish Houses of
     Parliament and Castletown House, Co. Kildare.

10   Sam Stephenson (b. Dublin; 1933–2006)
     Stephenson designed many of Dublin's notable buildings, including the Central Bank of
     Ireland, the ESB headquarters at Fitzwilliam Street, the Dublin Corporation Offices at
     Wood Quay and the Bord na Móna building, Baggot Street.

10 FASHION DESIGNERS

1 **Sybil Connolly (b. Swansea, Dublin-domiciled; 1921–98)**
Connolly designed Jacqueline Kennedy's dress for her official White House portrait.

2 **Paul Costelloe (b. Dublin; 1945–)**
Diana, Princess of Wales was a client of his.

3 **Irene Gilbert (b. Thurles, Co. Tipperary; 1910–85)**
Gilbert was Ireland's first couturier. She was known for her tweed daywear.

4 **Evelyn Gleeson (b. Cheshire; 1855–1944)**
A pioneering Celtic revival arts and crafts designer who established a plant in Dundrum, Dublin.

5 **Ib Jorgensen (b. Denmark, raised in Cavan; 1934–)**
Known for his work with his textile-designer wife Patricia Murray.

6 **Louise Kennedy (b. Dublin; 1960–)**
Mary Robinson chose to wear Louise Kennedy for her inauguration in 1990. Her other famous clients include Meryl Streep, Gwyneth Paltrow and Kylie Minogue.

7 **Richard Lewis (b. Dublin; 1945–)**
He is associated with the Private Lives collection in the Brown Thomas department store.

8 **Peter O'Brien (b. London, raised in Finglas, Dublin; 1954–)**
O'Brien worked with Dior, Givenchy and Rocha before returning to Dublin.

9 **John Rocha (b. Hong Kong, based in Dublin; 1953–)**
Rocha received a CBE in 2002 for his contribution to the fashion industry.

10 **Philip Treacy (b. Ballinasloe, Co. Galway; 1966–)**
Treacy is one of the world's most famous milliners. He created the hats for the wedding of HRH Prince of Wales and the Duchess of Cornwall.

MOST-CAUGHT FISH

	Type	Amount in tonnes*
1	Mackerel	72,345
2	Blue whiting	61,470
3	Farmed shellfish	43,092
4	Horse mackerel	37,431
5	Herring	33,178
6	Farmed finfish	15,263
7	Crab	14,429
8	Farmed salmon	14,067
9	Pilchard	12,997
10	Dublin Bay prawns	6,790

* Figures for 2007
Source: Central Statistics Office Ireland

HIGHEST TRADE SURPLUSES

	Year	Surplus in €m
1	2009	38,688
2	2002	38,047
3	2001	35,306
4	2004	33,304
5	2003	33,211
6	2005	29,267
7	2008	28,810
8	2000	27,980
9	2006	25,915
10	2007	25,740

Source: Central Statistics Office Ireland

Ireland ran just one trade surplus in the first 63 years after independence. It has subsequently run a trade surplus for 25 successive years.

TOP 10

EXPORT MARKETS

	Country	Trade in €bn*
1	USA	16.7
2	Britain	14.3
3	Belgium	12.1
4	Germany	6.1
5	France	4.9
6	Spain	3.6
7=	Italy	3
=	Netherlands	3
9	Switzerland	2.5
10	China	2.3

* Figures for 2008
Source: Central Statistics Office Ireland

TOP 10

IMPORT SOURCES

	Country	Trade in €bn*
1	Britain	17.9
2	USA	6.7
3	Germany	4.6
4	China	4.2
5	Netherlands	2.9
6	France	2.3
7=	Belgium	1.3
=	Italy	1.3
9	Norway	1.2
10	Japan	1.1

* Figures for 2008
Source: Central Statistics Office Ireland

FACTS ABOUT THE REPUBLIC OF IRELAND'S PLACE IN EUROPE

1   Highest proportion of population under 65.

2   Second highest income per head GDP per capita.

3   Third worst student-teacher ratio.

4   Fourth highest income based on GNI.

5   Fifth highest for greenhouse gas emissions.

6   Sixth highest level of mobile-phone penetration.

7   Seventh highest expenditure on education as percentage of GDP.

8   Eighth highest proportion of PhDs per heads of population aged 25–34.

9   Eleventh lowest proportion of GDP spent on healthcare.

10 Tenth highest level of internet access.

TOP 10

BESTSELLING MAKES OF CAR
in the Republic of Ireland*

1   Toyota

2   Ford

3   Volkswagen

4   Opel

5   Nissan

6   Renault

7   BMW

8   Peugeot

9   Hyundai

10 Audi

* In 2008
Source: Central Statistics Office Ireland

LARGEST TRADE UNIONS

	Union	Number of members*
1	Services, Industrial, Professional and Technical Union	216,881
2	IMPACT	61,450
3	Amicus/Unite	56,000
4	Amalgamated Transport and General Workers Union	47,163
5	Northern Ireland Public Service Alliance	45,506
6	Mandate	45,206
7	Technical Engineering and Electrical Union	45,035
8	Irish Nurses Organisation	40,100
9	Irish National Teachers Organisation	39,347
10	UNISON	39,100

* Figures for 2008
Source: Irish Congress of Trade Unions

TOP 10

SMALLEST TRADE UNIONS

	Union	Number of members*
1	Association of Irish Traditional Musicians	170
2	National Union of Rail, Maritime and Transport Workers	174
3	Equity	308
4	Veterinary Officers Association	325
5	First Division Civil Servants	362
6	Bakers Food and Allied Workers Union	500
7	Sales Marketing and Administrative Union of Ireland	520
8	Connect	566
9	Broadcasting Entertainment Cinematography and Theatre Union	580
10	Dairy Executives Association	700

* Figures for 2008
Source: Irish Congress of Trade Unions

LARGEST COMPANIES IN 1885

	Company	Business
1	Arthur Guinness Brewery	Brewery
2	York Street Flax Spinning Co.	Spinning
3	Thomas Gallaher's Tobacco	Tobacco
4	William Ewart & Son Ltd	Linen manufacture
5	John Arnott & Company	Retail and other interests
6	Edward Harland & Gustav Wilhelm Wolff	Ship builders
7	W. & R. Jacob Ltd	Biscuit manufacture
8	Samuel Davidson's Sirocco Rope Works	Rope manufacture
9	Ulster Spinning Company	Spinning
10	Bank of Ireland	Banking

Compiled from House of Commons list of largest ratepayers

Transport companies and utilities were the largest companies in Ireland in 1885, but when seven companies (the Great Southern and Western Railway Company, the Great Northern Railway Company, the Midland Great Western Railway Company, the Belfast and Northern Counties Railway, the Alliance & Dublin Consumers Gas Company, the Dublin Port and Docks Board and the Dublin Tramways Company) are eliminated from the list of largest companies, we get an idea of the demographics of Irish manufacturing industry and the profound effect it had on the politics of the time.

TOP 10
LARGEST COMPANIES IN 1975

	Company	Business	Turnover (IR£m)
1	An Bord Bainne	Agrifood	97.3
2	Smurfit	Packaging	78.5
3	Carrolls	Tobacco	77.6
4	Cement Roadstone	Construction supplier	77.4
5	Cork Marts	Livestock	76
6	Fitzwilton	Holdings	64.5
7	Mitchelstown	Agrifood	49
8	Brooks Watson	Holdings	46.9
9	Clover Meats	Agrifood	45.5
10	Waterford Glass	Glassware manufacture	45

Source: *Business & Finance*

LARGEST COMPANIES IN 1980

	Company	Business	Turnover (IR£m)
1	ESB	Electricity supplier	402.3
2	J. Smurfit Group	Packaging	401.4
3	Guinness Ireland	Beverage	352.6
4	CRH	Construction supplier	301.2
5	T&T	Construction	293.3
6	Esso Teo	Petrochemicals	287.6
7	Aer Lingus	Airline	272
8	Dunnes Stores	Retail	265
9	Irish Shell	Petrochemicals	253.1
10	Texaco	Petrochemicals	204.5

Source: *Business & Finance*

LARGEST COMPANIES IN 2008

	Company	Business	Turnover (€m)
1	CRH	Construction supplier	20,887
2	Dell Ireland	Technology	11,316
3	Microsoft Ireland	Technology	11,300
4	Smurfit Kappa	Packaging	7,062
5	DCC	Distribution	5,532
6	Intel Ireland	Technology	5,500
7	Google Ireland	Technology	5,280
8	Musgrave	Retail	4,800
9	Kerry Group	Agrifood	4,791
10	Dunnes Stores	Retail	4,300

Source: *The Irish Times* Top 1000 Companies

Northern Ireland's biggest company, Veridian, is in 35th place with a turnover of €1,590, while Tesco NI is in 53rd place with a turnover of €1,125. The combined turnover for the island would lift Tesco to 11th place.

TOP 10
LARGEST RETAILERS

1 Tesco

2 Dunnes Stores

3 Supervalu

4 Musgrave

5 SPAR

6 Superquinn

7 Aldi

8 Lidl

9 Centra

10 Marks & Spencer

Source: TNS Global Market Research

10 FAMOUS EXPORTS

1 Bailey's Irish Cream
This liqueur was an instant success upon its launch in 1974. In one month in 1978 it was responsible for 1 per cent of total exports.

2 Guinness Stout
Established as a brand in 1759, it was boosted by the removal of beer duty in 1795 and the Irish pound devaluation of 1797. A crisis in 1823 led the son of the founder to establish a new system of independent agents in English ports and cities that made Guinness the world's largest brewery by 1855.

3 Jameson Whiskey
Ireland's best-known whiskey brand was built up over a decade between 1810 and 1820 by John Jameson (1740–1823).

4 Linen
The collapse in the price of cotton in 1867 caused by the American Civil War led to the rise of the Irish linen industry, led by William Ewart, John Mulholland and others. Production peaked in 1870.

5 Marcus Ward's greetings cards
The most prominent designer of greetings cards of its era, the company also published children's books. However, 1,400 master craftsmen were made redundant when it folded abruptly in 1899, eight years after its founder's death.

6 Roe's Whiskey
George Roe's distillery, next door to Guinness's, sent out Ireland's largest export in the early 1800s.

7 Sirocco
Samuel Davison's tea-drying works in Belfast employed over 1,000 people by 1914.

8   Watt's Whiskey
     The largest distillery in the world dominated the Irish whiskey market before prohibition
     in America.

9   Wool
     Wool was Ireland's largest single export in the 18th century. English attempts to block
     exports from Ireland led to the parliamentary revolt of 1786 and to the 1798 revolution.

10   Viagra
     Ireland's biggest export of the 2000s was manufactured by Pfizer in Ringaskiddy and was
     responsible for 1 per cent of total exports in 1999.

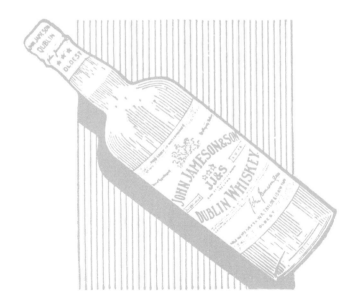

LARGEST FINANCIAL HOUSES*

1   DEPFA Bank

2   Bank of Ireland

3   Merrill Lynch International

4   Allied Irish Bank (AIB)

5   Anglo Irish Bank

6   Ulster Bank

7   Irish Life and Permanent

8   Central Bank of Ireland

9   J. P. Morgan Dublin

10 Irish Life Assurances

* In 2008, in terms of turnover

POLITICS AND
POLITICIANS

10
CLOSE ELECTION CALLS

1   **1965 Patrick Lenihan (FF) vs. Seán Mac Eoin (FG)**
    In Longford, Lenihan won by 13 votes after a count that took seven days, having initially
    been declared the winner by six. Lenihan's son Brian was already a minister, his daughter
    Mary O'Rourke subsequently became one, as did two of his grandchildren – Brian and
    Conor.

2   **1965 Denis Larkin (LAB) vs. Eugene Timmons (FF)**
    Larkin won by four votes after six days of counting in Dublin North East, having won by
    11 after the first count. An additional 145 spoiled votes were found on the recount.

3   **2010 Michele Gildernew (SF) vs. Rodney Connor (Unionist)**
    Gildernew was eight votes behind after the first count, 10 votes ahead after a recount, two
    votes ahead after a second recount and eventually elected by four votes on the third recount
    under the British first-past-the-post system. Gildernew had won the seat in 2001 by
    53 votes.

4   **1987 Dick Spring (LAB) vs. Tom McEllistrim (FF)**
    Spring's vote in Kerry North dropped by 3,000 but he held on and defeated McEllistrim for
    the fifth seat by five votes. A recount narrowed the margin to four votes and he was
    declared elected at 5 a.m.

5   **1989 Jim Fitzsimons (FF) vs. Michael Bell (LAB)**
    Fitzsimons won by ten, but his margin increased to 127 after an 11-hour recount in the
    Leinster European constituency. Bell unsuccessfully petitioned the High Court to have
    3,586 votes recounted – the voters had continued their preferences from the General
    Election ballot paper.

6   **1992 Eric Byrne (DL) vs. Ben Briscoe (FF)**
    Briscoe won by five votes after ten days of counting in Dublin South Central. He originally
    won by nine votes, then Byrne won the first recount by ten votes, then Briscoe won the sec-
    ond and third recounts by five votes.

7   **1997 John Gormley (GP) vs. Michael McDowell (PD)**
    Gormley was elected by 27 after eight days of counting in Dublin South East.

8   **2002 Mildred Fox (I) vs. Nicky Kelly (LAB)**
Fox won by 19 in a recount result declared for Wicklow eight days after polling. The first count was halted when Fox was ahead by 47. She won the first count by five.

9   **2002 John Dennehy (FF) vs. Kathy Sinnott (I)**
Initially Sinnott won by three votes (out of a total of 55,240 cast), but lost a first recount by two votes and a second recount by six votes in Cork South Central. The count took five days.

10   **2007 Brendan Ryan (LAB) vs. Clare Daly (SOC)**
Daly was 11 ahead after the first count but lost the nine-hour recount by two and was eliminated in Dublin North.

**DL – Democratic Left, GP – Green Party, FF – Fianna Fáil, FG – Fine Gael;
I – Independent, LAB – Labour, PD – Progressive Democrats; SOC – Socialist Party**

BIGGEST VOTE-GETTERS IN DÁIL ELECTIONS

	Candidate	Year	Constituency	Votes
1	Richard Mulcahy	1923	Dublin North	22,205
2	Kevin O'Higgins	1923	Dublin County	20,821
3	Jack Lynch	1977	Cork City	20,079
4	Eamon de Valera*	1933	Clare	18,574
5	Alfred Byrne	1932	Dublin North	18,170
6	W. T. Cosgrave*	1932	Cork Borough	18,125
7	Alfred Byrne	1927	Dublin North	17,780
8	Eithne Fitzgerald	1992	Dublin South	17,256
9	J. J. Walsh	1923	Cork Borough	17,151
10	Michael Collins	1922	Cork Mid, North, South, South-East and West	17,106

* Eamon de Valera scored 17,762 in 1923 and Cosgrave 17,795 in 1927 and 17,709 in 1923 in a different constituency, Carlow Kilkenny. This list shows the highest number of votes ever achieved by ten individual candidates

Ideally a politician should poll as close to the quota as possible, as the surplus is distributed proportionately and is far less valuable than a vote given to a party colleague. However, vote management was less evolved in the early days of the state so some of the totals were extraordinarily high. Eamon de Valera's total in 1923, for example, was three times the quota and his transfers managed to elect his colleague Brian O'Higgins, who finished bottom of the poll with just 114 votes.

The highest individual poll by any politician was 43,671 by Cecil Lavery in the Dublin by-election of 18 June 1935, but rules in by-elections, where there may be just two candidates, apply differently.

GROUNDBREAKING FEMALE LEADERS

1   Louie Bennett (b. Dublin, 1870–1956)
    Bennett was the founder of the Irishwomen's Suffrage Federation and the first ever female
    president of the Irish Congress of Trade Unions.

2   Kathleen Clarke (b. Limerick, 1878–1972)
    She was the wife of 1916 Rebellion leader Thomas Clarke and the first female Lord Mayor
    of Dublin.

3   Maud Gonne MacBride (b. London, 1866–1953)
    MacBride was a revolutionary who was the subject of more than 80 poems by W. B. Yeats.

4   Mary McAleese (b. Belfast, 1951–)
    McAleese became the Republic of Ireland's eighth president in 1997 and the first to have
    come from Northern Ireland.

5   Bernadette Devlin McAliskey (b. Cookstown, Co. Tyrone, 1947–)
    An activist in the Northern Ireland civil rights movement, she was elected to Westminster
    at the age of 22.

6   Josephine McNeill (b. Fermoy, Co. Cork, 1895–1969)
    She was one of the first female ambassadors in Europe. McNeill served as Irish ambassador
    to the Netherlands and Sweden in the 1950s.

7   Constance Markievicz (b. Sligo, 1868–1927)
    Markievicz was a leader of the 1916 Rebellion. She became Ireland's first female cabinet
    minister and was the first woman to be elected to the British Parliament, although she did
    not take her seat.

8   Fanny Parnell (b. Avondale, Co. Wicklow, 1848–82)
    Parnell was a poet and foundress of the Ladies Land League.

9   Mary Robinson (b. Ballina, Co. Mayo, 1944–)
    She was the Republic of Ireland's first female president, serving from 3 December 1990 to
    12 September 1997. She was the UN High Commissioner for Human Rights from
    September 1997 to September 2002.

10 Jennie Wyse Power (b. Baltinglass, Co. Wicklow, 1858–1941)
    Wyse Power was a political activist, suffragette and senator.

SHORTEST BUDGET SPEECHES

	Year	Minister for Finance	Number of words
1	1923	Ernest Blythe	3,934
2	1933	Seán MacEntee	5,620
3	1958	James Ryan	5,988
4	2002	Charlie McCreevy	6,095
5	2003	Charlie McCreevy	6,151
6	1924	Ernest Blythe	6,708
7	1947	Frank Aiken	7,002
8	1948	Patrick McGilligan	7,069
9	2004	Brian Cowen	7,099
10	2001	Charlie McCreevy	7,276

Word counts include interruptions, which sometimes delayed the delivery of the budget speech. Fast-talking Charlie McCreevy delivered three of the shortest budget speeches on record. Budget day was traditionally in April or May; however, it was moved to March temporarily in 1966, to January in 1975 and eventually to December in 1998.

LONGEST BUDGET SPEECHES

	Year	Minister for Finance	Number of words
1	1994	Bertie Ahern	20,950
2	1982	John Bruton	18,022
3	1990	Albert Reynolds	17,867
4	1980	Michael O'Kennedy	17,659
5	1992	Bertie Ahern	17,167
6	1977	Richie Ryan	17,097
7	1976	Richie Ryan	16,806
8	1975	Richie Ryan	16,794
9	1993	Bertie Ahern	16,397
10	1970	Jack Lynch	16,382

Bertie Ahern and Richie Ryan have each delivered three of the longest budget speeches in history.

Jack Lynch delivered the 1970 budget in the absence of Charles Haughey, the Minister for Finance at the time, who had been injured, allegedly, in a fall from a horse the day before the budget.

Apart from being the second-longest budget speech in history, the 1982 budget precipitated the fall of the coalition government.

10 FAMOUS POLITICAL NICKNAMES

	Nickname	Real name
1	The Big Fellow	Michael Collins
2	Big Ian	Ian Paisley
3	The Blacksmith of Ballinalee	Seán Mac Keon
4	The Bull	John Donoghue
5	The Chief	Charles Haughey
6	The Long Fellow	Eamon de Valera
7	Ho Chi Quinn	Ruairi Quinn
8	Minister for Hardship	Liam Cosgrave
9	Minister for Snow	Michael O'Leary
10	Richie Ruin	Richie Ryan

Michael O'Leary was also known as 'The Thawnaiste'; this was as a result of the wintry weather in 1982.

REFERENDUM RESULTS

	Year	Referendum	Vote	Outcome
1	1937	New Constitution	57–43	Yes
2	1958	First past the post electoral system	48–52	No*
3	1972	Join European Community	83–17	Yes
4	1972	Reduce voting age to 18	85–15	Yes
5	1983	Constitutional prohibition on abortion	67–33	Yes†
6	1986	Remove constitutional restriction on divorce	37–63	No‡
7	1999	Good Friday Agreement (Republic)	94–6	Yes
8	1999	Good Friday Agreement (North)	71–29	Yes
9	2002	Nice Treaty	46–54	No§
10	2008	Lisbon Treaty	46.6–53.4	No**

* Re-put in 1968, 39–61, No

† Further attempts to restrict travel for abortion in 1992 resulted 65–35, No; abortion information in 2002 resulted in 49.6–50.4, No

‡ Re-put in 1996, 50.3–49.7, Yes

§ Re-put in 2002, 63–37, Yes

** Re-put in 2009, 67–33, Yes

SUPREME COURT DECISIONS

1 **1943**
Found against act empowering the minister to certify the standard of private education.
(School Attendance Act)

2 **1950**
Found that the Constitution guarantees the right to private property. (*Buckley* case)

3 **1950**
Found that both parents have equal rights in the upbringing of children. (*Tilson* case)

4 **1973**
Found that it is unconstitutional to prohibit the importation of contraceptives. (*McGee* case)

5 **1976**
Found that women's rights to equality on issues like jury service were guaranteed by the Constitution. (*de Burca* case)

6 **1978**
Found that the government acted illegally in dismissing Garda Commissioner Edmund Garvey following his refusal to resign. (*Garvey* case)

7 **1983**
Found that criminalization of homosexuality was legal under the Constitution. (*Norris* case, homosexuality was decriminalized shortly afterwards)

8 **1992**
Found that women at risk of suicide were entitled to abortion. (*X* case)

9 **1995**
Found that both sides in a referendum are entitled to equal funding. (*McKenna* case)

10 **2006**
Found that a declaration that a law is unconstitutional does not retrospectively invalidate all actions taken under it. (*A* case)

TRIBUNALS OF INQUIRY

Inquiry/chair

1 **Barr/Robert Barr**
Established in 2000 to investigate the 'facts and circumstances' surrounding the fatal shooting of John Carthy at Abbeylara.

2 **Flood/Feargus Flood**
Established in October 1997 after Minister Ray Burke admitted accepting 'political donations' from building developers.

3 **Lindsay/Alison Lindsay**
Established in September 1999 to investigate the infection of 260 haemophiliacs with HIV and hepatitis C.

4 **Locke's/John O'Byrne, Kevin Haugh, Cahir Davitt**
Established in 1947 to find out if international swindler Alexander Maximoe had bribed politicians to purchase the ailing Locke's distillery in Kilbeggan, or, more likely, its 60,000 gallons of matured whiskey. It found he hadn't.

5 **McCracken/Brian McCracken**
Established in 1997 to inquire into alleged payments to politicians by Ben Dunne. The report led to the Moriarty Tribunal.

6 **Mahon/Alan Mahon**
Established in 1997 to look at payments made relating to developments in the Greater Dublin region and the contract for Century Radio.

7 **Money-lending/Sean Butler, Denis Pringle, Cathal Ó Floinn**
Established in 1970 to inquire into illegal money-lending following an exposé on RTÉ's *Seven Days* programme. It criticized the programme-makers for exaggerating the problem.

8 **Moriarty/Michael Moriarty**
Established in September 1997 to inquire into payments made to Charles Haughey and Michael Lowry.

9 **Morris/Frederick Morris**
Established in 2002 to inquire into garda behaviour in Donegal. It found that a sergeant had planted a shotgun at a Travellers' encampment at Burnfoot.

10 **Scarman/Leslie Scarman**
Established in 1969 to investigate the cause of disturbances in Northern Ireland.

FAMOUS MEMBERS OF THE 18TH-CENTURY IRISH PARLIAMENT

1   **Jonah Barrington (1760–1834)**
    He is most famous for the two colourful memoirs of 18th-century society and politics that
    he wrote after he was removed from office for embezzlement.

2   **Henry Boyle (1684–1764)**
    The most powerful Speaker of the Parliament, he eventually had to be bought off with a
    pension of £30,000 and the title of Earl of Shannon.

3   **Alan Brodrick (1660–1728)**
    Twice the Speaker, he was a champion of penal laws and a thorn in the side of the colonial
    regime.

4   **William Conolly (1662–1729)**
    This Donegal-born parliamentary fixer became Speaker of the House and was the first of
    the 'undertakers'*.

5   **John Philpot Curran (1750–1817)**
    He was a duellist, literary figure and raconteur who served as the defence lawyer for the
    United Irishmen after the 1798 Rebellion. His daughter had an affair with Robert Emmet.

6   **Ralph Gore (1675–1733)**
    This Donegal MP took over Conolly's roll as Speaker.

7   **Henry Grattan (1746–1820)**
    Grattan was a rigorous defender of free trade and Irish parliamentary independence.
    Although he was always on the opposition benches, the Parliament became known as
    'Grattan's Parliament'.

8   **John Ponsonby (1713–89)**
    A Speaker who proclaimed 'Let us stick to our own circle and manage our own little game
    as well as we can.'

9   Boyle Roche (1743–1807)

Roche was famous for his nonsensical quotes: 'A man cannot be in two places at once unless he is a bird.'

10   Thomas 'Buck' Whaley (1766–1800)

He was a notorious gambler who whittled away a fortune of £400,000 and contracted debts of £30,000. He won a bet by playing handball against the Wall of Jerusalem.

* In the absence of a party system, Irish politics in the 18th century was dominated by 'undertakers' who 'undertook' to get legislation through the house for the English crown with bribes and promises of career advancement for their followers

10
PARLIAMENTARY CONSTITUENCIES IN GRATTAN'S TIME

1 Ardfert, Co. Kerry

2 Askeaton, Co. Limerick

3 Baltimore, Co. Cork

4 Belturbet, Co. Cavan

5 Clonakilty, Co. Cork

6 Fore, Co. Westmeath

7 Harristown, Co. Kildare

8 Innisteague, Co. Monaghan

9 Newcastle, Co. Dublin

10 Randalstown, Co. Meath.

The Irish parliament had 300 members for much of the 18th century. Many of them were returned by small and obscure constituencies: 200 members were elected by 100 individuals and nearly 50 by 10. The Boyle family returned 16 members, the Ponsonby family 14, the Hill family 9 and the FitzGerald family 7.

PEOPLE WHO MIGHT HAVE
SHOT MICHAEL COLLINS

1   **Robert 'Bobs' Doherty**
When he arrived in the USA in 1925, he claimed to have been the man who shot Collins.

2   **Sean Galvin**
Brought the word to the Anti-Free State meeting in a nearby house that Collins had been shot, and later claimed to have shot Collins himself.

3   **Pete Kearney**
Told a priest that he had fired a single shot at a man on the road during the ambush.

4   **Tom Kelleher**
The man blamed by Garda Sergeant John Hickey in his official inquiry.

5   **John McPeak**
Machine-gunner on the armoured car accompanying Collins who later defected to the Republicans.

6   **Joe Murphy**
A Lissarda man from another brigade who said on the evening of the ambush that he thought he might have shot Collins.

7   **Dan O'Connor**
Said to have been court-martialled for shooting Collins.

8   **Denis 'Sonny' O'Neill**
Ex-British Army marksman who claimed to have shot Collins after the ambush.

9   **Jimmy Ormond**
Claimed in 1926 that he fired directly at Collins with a Lee Enfield and saw him fall.

10 **James Sheehan**
A student who was with Bobs Doherty; he disappeared after the ambush.

After 40 books, dozens of documentaries and over 1,000 articles on the subject, there is still great confusion over the events of 22 August 1922, the ambush at Bealnablath and the identity of the killer of Michael Collins. The results of the official investigation into the shooting were destroyed by the outgoing Cumann na Gaedheal government in 1932.

10 IRISH-BORN PRIME MINISTERS OF OTHER STATES/COUNTRIES

	Name/Dates	Where born	Term in office	State/country
1	Frederick Alderdice (1872–1936)	Belfast	1928, 1932–4	Newfoundland
2	John Ballance (1839–93)	Glenavy	1891–3	New Zealand
3	Charles Gavan Duffy (1816–1903)	Monaghan	1871–2	Victoria
4	Patrick Jennings (1831–97)	Newry	1886–7	New South Wales
5	Bryan O'Loghlen (1828–1905)	Ruan	1881–3	Victoria
6	John O'Shanassy (1818–83)	Ballinahow	1857, 1858–9, 1861–3	Victoria
7	Arthur Palmer (1819–98)	Armagh	1870–74	Queensland
8	Daniel Pollen (1813–96)	Dublin	1875–6	New Zealand
9	Robert Torrens (1814–84)	Cork	1857	South Australia
10	Arthur Wellesley (1769–1852)	Dublin	1828–30, 1834	Great Britain

THE SPORTING ISLE

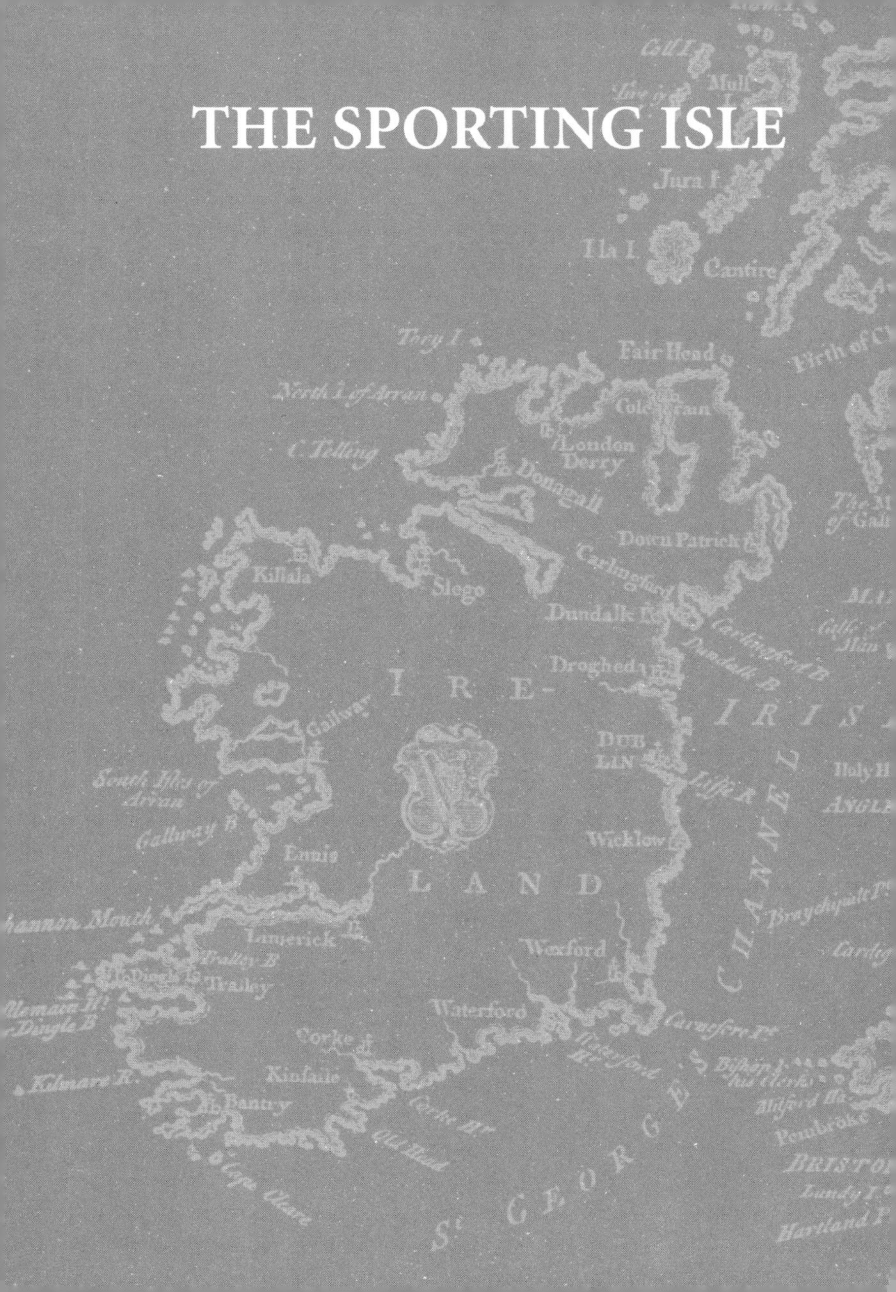

WORLD CHAMPIONS

	Champion	Sport	Year(s)
1	Paul Brady	Handball singles	2003, 2006, 2009
2	Sue Carey	Handball singles	1986
3	Eamonn Coghlan	5000 m	1983
4	Ken Doherty	Snooker	1997
5	Sonia O'Sullivan	5000 m	1995
6	Stephen Roche	Cycling	1987
7	Fiona Shannon	Handball singles	2003, 2006, 2009
8	Tim Smythe	Cross country	1931
9	Dennis Taylor	Snooker	1985
10	John Treacy	Cross country	1978, 1979

Sonia O'Sullivan also won the World Cross Country title in 1998.

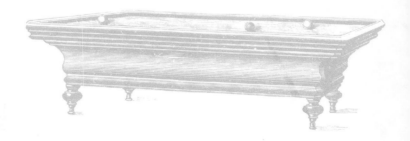

FORGOTTEN WORLD CHAMPIONS

	Champion	Sport	Year(s)
1	Alexandra Betham	Archery	1864–9
2	Steve Casey	NWA Heavyweight Wrestling	1938–9
3	Cyril Corbally	Croquet	1902, 1903, 1906, 1908, 1913
4	Peter Corcoran	Prize fighting	1771–6
5	George Dockrell	100 m freestyle	1909
6	Dan Dougherty	Prize fighting	1813
7	Peter Duff Matthews	Croquet	1914, 1919, 1920, 1927
8	Eddie Heron	Diving	1933
9	Leslie O'Callaghan	Croquet	1910, 1912, 1921
10	Dan O'Mahoney	NWA Heavyweight Wrestling	1935–6

Some of these events are no longer regarded as world championship status, although they were de facto world championships in their time.

OLYMPIC STORIES

1   **1900 Paris Summer Olympics**
     John Flanagan (b. Kilbreedy, Co. Limerick; 1873–1938)
     Flanagan won the first of his three successive Olympic gold medals in the hammer. He was the most successful of a group of weight-throwers called the 'Irish whales'.

2   **1904 St. Louis Summer Olympics**
     Thomas F. Kiely (b. Ballyneale, Co. Tipperary; 1869–1951)
     He paid his own way to the St. Louis Olympics as he was determined to compete for Ireland rather than the Great Britain team. He won the first Olympic decathlon.

3   **1906 Athens Intercalated Games**
     Peter O'Connor (b. Co. Wicklow; 1872–1957)
     The world long-jump record holder was one of three athletes who went to the intercalated games in Athens to represent Ireland only to find that they were listed as British team members. When he won a silver medal he climbed the flagpole with an Irish flag.

4   **1928 Amsterdam Summer Olympics**
     Pat O'Callaghan (b. Kanturk, Co. Cork; 1906–91)
     O'Callaghan became Ireland's first gold medallist since independence, in the hammer.

5   **1932 Los Angeles Summer Olympics**
     Bob Tisdall (b. Sri Lanka; 1907–2004)
     Raised in Nenagh, Co. Tipperary, he was given special dispensation to qualify for the Olympics at the second attempt. He won gold in the 400-m hurdles. Within an hour Pat O'Callaghan won the hammer, his second Olympic gold. This was a special day for the Irish team.

6   **1956 Melbourne Summer Olympics**
     Ronnie Delany (b. Arklow, Co. Wicklow; 1935–)
     Delany struggled to qualify for the Olympics, but he made it to the 1500-m final. Australia's John Landy was the favourite for the big race. Delany kept close to Landy until the final lap. When Landy realized he could not win, he ushered through Delany, who used his trademark final sprint to win.

7   **1972 Munich Summer Olympics**
     Mary Peters (b. Belfast; 1939–)
     One of the great duels in Olympic history, Mary Peters beat the local athlete Heide Rosendahl to win the pentathlon gold medal.

8   1984 Los Angeles Summer Olympics
     John Treacy (b. Villierstown, Co. Waterford; 1957–)
     Treacy isolated himself from the rest of the Ireland team in the Olympic village to
     prepare for the marathon. The double World Cross Country champion ran the race of
     his life to win the silver medal.

9   2000 Sydney Summer Olympics
     Sonia O'Sullivan (b. Cobh, Co. Cork; 1969–)
     Following the disappointment of finishing fourth in the 3000 m in Barcelona in 1992
     and failing to finish in the 5000 m in Atlanta in 1996 because of an upset stomach, she
     took silver in the 5000 m in Sydney.

10   2002 Salt Lake City Winter Olympics
     Clifton Wrottesley (b. Galway; 1968–)
     The closest Ireland has come to a medal at the Winter Olympics was when Wrottesley
     finished fourth in the skeleton in 2002. He served as Chef de Mission for the Irish team
     in 2006.

10 SUMMER OLYMPICS NEAR MISSES

	Games	Competitor	Event
1	1932 Los Angeles	Eamonn Fitzgerald	Triple jump
2	1956 Melbourne	Gerald Martina	Light-heavyweight wrestling
3	1960 Rome	John Lawlor	Hammer
4	1964 Tokyo	Ireland team	Three-day event
5	1976 Montreal	Eamonn Coghlan	1500 m
6	1976 Montreal	Sean Drea	Single sculls (rowing)
7	1992 Barcelona	Sonia O'Sullivan	3000 m
8	1996 Atlanta	Ireland team	Lightweight coxless four (rowing)
9	2004 Athens	Kevin Babington	Showjumping
10	2008 Bejing	Eoin Rheinisch	Canoe slalom

All of these competitors finished just out of the medals in fourth place.

Eamonn Coghlan finished fourth again at the 1980 Moscow Olympics, this time in the 5000 m.

GREATEST EVER SPORTSPEOPLE

1   Pádraig Harrington (Golfer)

2   Paul McGrath (Soccer player)

3   Vincent O'Brien (Racehorse trainer)

4   Christy Ring (Hurler)

5   Sonia O'Sullivan (Athlete)

6   Sean Kelly (Cyclist)

7   Roy Keane (Soccer player)

8   George Best (Soccer players)

9   Joey Dunlop (Motorcyclist)

10 Brian O'Driscoll (Rugby player)

As voted on RTÉ, 31 December 2009

RECORD-BREAKING YEARS FOR ATHLETICS

1   **1861**
Three world records were broken on grass tracks in the space of two months. James Heaviside from Donabate ran the mile in 4 mins 55 secs and eight weeks later he improved on his own time, reducing it to 4 mins 49 secs. Then Matthew Greene ran a new record of 4 mins 46 secs at Trinity College.

2   **1862**
George Farran, a student from Artane, ran the mile in 4 mins 33 secs.

3   **1873**
Andrew C. Courtney won the 1000 yd in 2 mins 23.6 secs at Dublin University Sports in College Park. It was later claimed as the first recognized world record.

4   **1880**
Keeping it in the family, Pat Davin took the world high-jump record from his brother Tom at Carrick-on-Suir in Knocknaconnery. Three years later he set a world long-jump record at Monasterevin. Until his high-jump record was broken by American William Byrd-Page in 1885, he held both the world long- and high-jump records, the only man in history to do so.

5   **1885**
Two Irish athletes set world records in this year. J. C. Daly of the GAA set the record in the triple jump with a distance of 13 m 51 cm (44 ft 4 in). William Barry of the IAAA set a world hammer record in Tralee. He went on to improve on it eight times in three years.

6   **1893**
Tommy Conneff, from Clane, Co. Kildare, ran a world mile record of 4 mins 17.8 secs. Two years later he reduced it to 4 mins 15.6 secs and this record remained unbeaten for 16 years.

7   **1895**
Conneff set the world record for the three-quarter mile, with a time of 3 mins 2.8 secs. This record stood until 1931. Kilmallock-born John Flanagan threw the hammer 44.45 m (145 ft 8 in) at the GAA Championship in Clonmel. He went on to extend the record 14 times in a 14-year period.

8   **1897**
    IAAA athlete W. J. M. Newburn set a world long-jump record of 4 m 28 cm (14 ft ½ in)
    in Dublin.

9   **1900**
    Peter O'Connor set a new long-jump world record with a distance of 7.49 m (24½ ft). He
    reduced it to 7.59 m (25 ft) a year later. It remained a world long-jump record for 20 years
    and an Irish national record until 1990.

10 **1937**
    Pat O'Callaghan threw a world record for the hammer, 59.54 m (195 ft 4¾ in). His record
    stood until 1949 when the record left Ireland for the first time.

GRAND DAMS OF RACING

1   Ballinode
This Sligo mare won the second ever running of the Cheltenham Gold Cup in 1925 for trainer Frank Morgan.

2   Blue Wind
She won the 1981 Epsom Oaks, the 'Derby for Fillies', and this victory launched Dermot Weld's career as a champion flat trainer.

3   Dawn Run
This horse became a national hero after winning the 1986 Cheltenham Gold Cup. Two years previously she won the Champion Hurdle, so she became the first horse to complete the Cheltenham Gold Cup/Champion Hurdle double.

4   Glencaraig Lady
A surprise winner of the 1972 Cheltenham Gold Cup, the horse was trained by Francis Flood and ridden by Frank Berry.

5   Jet Ski Lady
First past the post in the 1991 Epsom Oaks, Jet Ski Lady gave trainer Jim Bolger his first English Classic winner.

6   Long Look
Ridden by Jack Purtell, Long Look gave Vincent O'Brien his first victory in the Epsom Oaks in 1965.

7   Maid Of Athens
She was the first filly to win the Irish Derby, a feat she achieved in 1871.

8   Noblesse
Sister of Ballymoss, Noblesse became the first Irish-trained winner of the Epsom Oaks in 1963.

9   Rhodora
Richard Croker's Irish-American-bred mare, trained by Fred McCabe and then James Allen, won the 1,000 Guineas in 1908. Rhodora failed to win the Epsom Oaks in the same year when she was felled by a loose horse.

10   Shahtoush
Ridden by Michael Kinane and trained by Aidan O'Brien, Shahtoush came from behind to win the 1998 Epsom Oaks by ¾ length.

AINTREE WINNERS

	Year(s)	Horse	Odds	Jockey	Trainer
1	1850/ 1851	Abd-El-Kader	7/1	Chris Green/ Tom Abbott	Joseph Osborne
2	1953	Early Mist	20/1	Bryan Marshall	Vincent O'Brien
3	1954	Royal Tan	8/1	Bryan Marshall	Vincent O'Brien
4	1955	Quare Times	100/9	Pat Taaffe	Vincent O'Brien
5	1958	Mr What	18/1	Arthur Freeman	Tom Taaffe
6	1999	Bobbyjoe	10/1	Paul Carberry	Tommy Carberry
7	2000	Papillon	10/1	Ruby Walsh	Ted Walsh
8	2003	Monty's Pass	16/1	Barry Geraghty	Jimmy Mangan
9	2005	Hedgehunter	7/1	Ruby Walsh	Willie Mullins
10	2006	Numbersixvalverde	11/1	Niall Madden	Martin Brassil

CHELTENHAM HEROES

1 Arkle
Bred on the Meath side of the Kildare border near Maynooth, Arkle was raised and trained in north Dublin. His three Gold Cup wins in 1964–6, with Ardclough jockey Pat Taaffe on board, made him the first four-legged celebrity of the TV age and a national hero.

2 Captain Christy
This 1974 Gold Cup winner was trained by Pat Taaffe, the jockey forever associated with Arkle.

3 Cottage Rake
Cork-bred and trained in Tipperary by the then unknown Vincent O'Brien, the Rake was famously spun by a vet three times before being bought by businessman Frank Viller. He won the Gold Cup three times in a row, from 1948–50.

4 Danoli
Danoli never won a championship race, but he was beloved for his small-town origins, unknown trainer and the fact that owner Dan O'Neill had never been on a plane before coming to watch him win the Sun Alliance Novices' Hurdle in 1994.

5   **Dawn Run**
This mare's heroic Gold Cup finish in 1986 clinched the double for trainer Paddy Mullins, as she had won the Champion Hurdle two years previously.

6   **Hatton's Grace**
Trained by Vincent O'Brien, Hatton's Grace was a triple Champion Hurdle champion from 1949–51.

7   **Imperial Call**
His 1996 win for Cork trainer Fergie Sutherland inspired the most chaotic winners' enclosure scrummage Cheltenham has ever seen.

8   **Istabraq**
A failed horse on the flat, Istabraq was converted into a hurdler through the genius of John Durkan. Unfortunately, Durkan did not live to see him win three successive Champion Hurdles from 1998–2000. Foot and mouth restrictions prevented him travelling to go for four in a row.

9   **L'Escargot**
Regarded as one of the greatest racehorses ever, L'Escargot was a double Gold Cup winner for trainer Dan Moore in 1970 and 1971. He followed up these victories by winning the 1975 Aintree Grand National.

10   **War of Attrition**
This horse's victory in the Gold Cup for trainer Mouse Morris in 2006 was famously celebrated by the owner, Ryanair boss Michael O'Leary, telling an English reporter, 'We keep the best stuff at home and sell you the rubbish'.

CHAMPION TRAINERS

1 ### Jim Bolger (1941–)
Born in Wexford and based in Carlow, Bolger has been a leading trainer since 1977. His successes include the Epsom Oaks with Jet Ski Lady in 1991 and the Epsom Derby with New Approach in 2008. These are just two examples of his many winners.

2 ### Tom Dreaper (1899–1975)
From Rathsallagh, Dreaper is the most successful trainer in the Cheltenham Gold Cup (seven wins, three by Arkle), and the Irish Grand National, which he won seven times. The gentleman always considered himself a farmer first and horse trainer second.

3 ### Fred McCabe (1868–1954)
When owner Richard Croker's Orby won the Epsom Derby in 1907 there was a rejoicing that 'a Catholic horse' had won England's derby.

4 ### Aidan O'Brien (1969–)
This Wexford-born trainer took over the well-funded Ballydoyle stable at the age of 27 in 1996 and was Ireland's third most successful trainer of all time by the age of 30. His successes include the Prix de l'Arc de Triomphe with Dylan Thomas in 2007, the Epsom Derby with Galileo in 2001 and High Chaparral in 2002, seven Irish Derbies and a record seven consecutive Group One races with Rock Of Gibraltar in 2002.

5 ### Vincent O'Brien (1917–2009)
Vincent O'Brien was the most successful trainer of his generation. Born in Cork and raised in Tipperary, among his many triumphs were four Cheltenham Gold Cups and three Champion Hurdles, the Prix de l'Arc de Triomphe with Ballymoss in 1958 and six Epsom Derbies with Larkspur in 1962, Sir Ivor in 1968, Nijinsky in 1970, Roberto in 1972, The Minstrel in 1977 and Golden Fleece in 1982.

6 ### John Oxx (1950–)
Based in Killabeg on The Curragh, his horse Ridgewood Pearl won the Breeders' Cup at Belmont Park, New York, in 1995. In 2009 Sea the Stars won six Group One races in six months, including the Prix de l'Arc de Triomphe and the Epsom Derby.

7   James J. Parkinson (1870–1948)

Born in Tramore, during his time as a jockey Parkinson went to America in 1902 while under suspension. He then settled in Maddenstown and became a serial Irish Champion Trainer. His record of 135 winners in 1923 stood until 1990.

8   Paddy J. Prendergast (1909–80)

This Curragh-born trainer's career started with just two horses and he had to travel round on his bicycle borrowing feed. He won all the Classics except the Epsom Derby, and became the first Irish trainer to become top trainer in Britain in successive years, 1963–6.

9   Mick Rogers (1925–85)

The third in a family line of famous Curragh trainers, his 1958 Epsom Derby victory with Hard Ridden made amends for his grandfather having Trigo moved to England before his victory in the 1929 Derby. Mick Rogers won the race again with Santa Claus in 1964.

10   Dermot Weld (1948–)

Weld was the first Irish trainer to win an American Classic. Go And Go won the Belmont Stakes in 1990. He had further international success in the Melbourne Cup, with Vintage Crop in 1993 and Media Puzzle in 2002. He trained 150 winners in 1991.

10 CHAMPION JOCKEYS

1   **Aubrey Brabazon (b. Kilcumney, Co. Kilkenny; 1920–96)**
Raised at the Ranger's Lodge on The Curragh, Brabazon rode 406 winners in Ireland between 1935 and 1959. He achieved a Cheltenham Gold Cup treble in 1948–50.

2   **Richard Dunwoody (b. Belfast; 1964–)**
Dunwoody rode a total of 1,699 winners in Britain during his career. He won the Champion Jockey title in England three times, 1993–5.

3   **Pat Eddery (b. Blackrock, Co. Dublin; 1952–)**
Eddery is the second most successful jockey of all time on the English flat circuit, with 4,632 wins. He was Champion Jockey in England 11 times, a three-time Derby winner and is co-holder of the record for the most wins in the Prix de l'Arc de Triomphe.

4   **Kieren Fallon (b. Crusheen, Co. Clare; 1965–)**
A six-time champion on the English flat circuit, Fallon has also won the Derby three times.

5   **Barry Geraghty (b. Drumcree, Co. Meath; 1979–)**
Geraghty was Irish Champion Jump Jockey in 2000 and 2004. He rode his 1,000th winner on 2 November 2009.

6   **Tony McCoy (b. Moneyglass, Co. Antrim; 1974–)**
McCoy has been dominant over the jumps on the British circuit since 1995. He has over 3,000 wins under National Hunt rules and has won the Champion Jockey title 15 times.

7   **Tim Molony (b. Croom, Co. Limerick; 1919–)**
Molony was the Champion Jockey over the jumps five times on the English circuit, 1949–52 and 1955.

8   **Jonjo O'Neill (b. Castletownroche, Co. Cork; 1952–)**
Champion Jockey over the jumps in England in 1978 and 1980, he rode Dawn Run to Cheltenham success in 1986.

9   **Tommy Stack (b. Moyvane, Co. Limerick; 1945–)**
Most remembered for his Grand National wins on Red Rum, Stack was the Champion Jockey on the English jump circuit in 1975 and 1977.

10   **Pat Taaffe (1930–92)**
His 25 wins at Cheltenham include riding Arkle to a Cheltenham Gold Cup treble in the 1960s.

FLAT CHAMPION HORSES

	Year		Trainer
1	1907	Orby	Fred McCabe
2	1958	Hard Ridden	Mick Rogers
3	1962	Larkspur	Vincent O'Brien
4	1964	Santa Claus	Mick Rogers
5	1968	Sir Ivor	Vincent O'Brien
6	1970	Nijinsky	Vincent O'Brien
7	1982	Golden Fleece	Vincent O'Brien
8	2002	High Chaparral	Aidan O'Brien
9	2008	New Approach	Jim Bolger
10	2009	Sea the Stars	John Oxx

SPORTING CONTROVERSIES

1   **1902**
The Gaelic Athletic Association (GAA) banned its members from playing rival football codes – soccer and rugby. This ban remained in place until 1971.

2   **1921**
When the Irish Cup semi-final between Glenavon and Shelbourne resulted in a draw, the Belfast-based Irish Football Association (IFA) insisted that the replay be played in Belfast. Shelbourne withdrew from the competition and were joined by Dublin clubs Bohemians and St James's Gate, and Belfast club Alton United, in forming a new soccer body, the Football Association of Ireland (FAI).

3   **1925**
An argument against the holding of greyhound races alongside foot races at a sports meet in Belfast caused a split within the National Athletics and Cycling Association (NACA) and eventually led to a breakaway Northern Ireland athletics body.

4   **1936**
English athletics official Harold Abrahams failed in his move to have the Irish NACA excluded from international athletics, but later had the decision forced through at committee level. The effect was that the majority of Irish athletes were prevented from competing internationally until 1967.

5   **1948**
The English organizing committee of the Olympic Games objected to the Irish team using the name 'Ireland' in the opening ceremony, and excluded the Irish team from the event.

6   **1948**
Belfast Celtic player Jimmy Jones was attacked after a soccer match and had his leg broken in several places. The Celtic club, the only one in Northern Ireland to have a Catholic support base, was forced to withdraw from soccer.

7   **1952**
Irish players from outside of Ulster objected to 'God Save the Queen' being played before their rugby match with Wales. No further internationals have been staged in Belfast.

8   1972
Scotland and Wales refused to play in Dublin because of increased tension caused by the massacre of civil rights demonstrators in Derry by the British Army. The international championship was incomplete.

9   1996
Michelle Smith won three gold medals and a bronze at the Atlanta Olympics but there were suspicions about the rapid progress she had made in the lead-up to the event. Eventually, in 1998, she was banned after a urine sample was found to be contaminated with alcohol and the bodybuilding drug androstenedione was also found in her sample. She claimed her samples had been interfered with.

10 2000
Cian O'Connor's horse Waterford Crystal tested positive for prohibited, but not performance-enhancing, substances following a gold medal-winning performance in showjumping at the Athens Olympics. He was stripped of the medal, and in a bizarre twist, a second blood sample was stolen from the offices of the Irish Equestrian Federation.

10

SPORTING DISASTERS

1   **1882 England 13 Ireland 0**
The most one-sided international in history was also Ireland's first ever soccer match.

2   **1972 A length to go**
The Irish Olympic 4 x 100-m freestyle swimming relay team of Anne O'Connor, Christine Fulcher, Brenda McGrory and Aisling O'Leary had a length of the pool still to complete when USA won the gold medal.

3   **1980 Pistol jam**
Ken Stanford, an RUC inspector competing for Ireland at the 1980 Olympics, found that his pistol had jammed and he had to carry out emergency repairs mid-competition.

4   **1980 Penalty points**
At the Moscow Olympics, Sackville Currie, a modern pentathlete, managed to incur a world record 2,000 penalty points by jumping the equestrian course backwards.

5   **1984 Demolition**
The Olympic hammer competition had to be delayed when Declan Hegarty released his hammer at the wrong point three times in succession and demolished the protective netting.

6   **1992 New Zealand 59 Ireland 6**
The All Blacks scored 11 tries in Wellington, eight in the second half, to conclude Ireland's heaviest ever rugby defeat. This was a week after they had run the home team to within three points in Dunedin.

7   **1996 Not ideal preparation**
Sonia O'Sullivan was a favourite for the Olympic 5000 m but a stomach upset that she had been suffering from in the lead-up caused her to fade out of the race. Earlier she was drawn into a sponsorship row when she had to change her gear on the way to the track.

8   2002 Soccer Fallout

Ireland's preparations for the World Cup were dominated by a falling out between Roy Keane and manager Mick McCarthy at the training camp in Saipan. Keane returned home before a ball was kicked.

9   2004 Unwanted record

Northern Ireland's soccer team set a new world record, 1,354 minutes, more than 13 games, without a goal. In the match against Poland the crowd counted down as the time for the record approached and then chanted 'champion-ez'.

10   2009 France 1 Ireland 1

Ireland led 1–0 in the Stade de France in extra time of the away leg of their World Cup play-off against France. However, on 104 minutes, Thierry Henry clearly handled the ball before passing it to William Gallas, who scored the equalizing goal. France qualified for the World Cup finals on the away-goal rule.

10
RECORD SPORTS ATTENDANCES

	Year	Event	Attendance
1	1868	First day of the Punchestown Festival (National Hunt racing)	150,000
2	1954	All-Ireland hurling final Cork vs. Wexford	84,856
3	1961	All-Ireland football final Down vs. Offaly	90,556
4	1967	North West 200 (Motorcycle race)	150,000
5	2006	All-Ireland women's football final Cork vs. Armagh	25,665
6	2009	Six Nations Championship Ireland vs. England (Rugby)	82,206
7	2009	World Cup 2010 play-off Republic of Ireland vs. France (Soccer)	74,103
8	2007	All-Ireland camogie final Wexford vs. Cork	33,154
9	2009	European Cup semi-final Munster vs. Leinster (Rugby)	82,208
10	2009	Volvo Ocean Race (Yacht race)	150,000

PLAYERS WITH THE MOST RUGBY CAPS

	Player	Caps*
1	John Hayes	97 (91+6)
2	Brian O'Driscoll	96 (95+1)
3	Ronan O'Gara	93 (76+17)
4	Malcolm O'Kelly	92 (80+12)
5	Peter Stringer	91 (79+12)
6	Girvan Dempsey	82 (68+14)
7	Fergus Slattery	73 (61+12)
8	David Humphreys	72 (44+28)
9	Kevin Maggs	70 (59+11)
10	Mike Gibson	69

* Figures represent starts + appearances as substitute up to the end of the 2010 six nations championship. Source: Irish Rugby Football Union

A Top 10 confined to players who started, in deference to those players who played before substitutions were allowed, would include Willie John McBride (63), Denis Hickie (62) and Shane Horgan (61+3).

10
NATIONAL RUGBY VICTORIES

1   **1887 Ireland 6 England 0**
     The first match at Lansdowne Road brought Ireland's first victory over England, by two converted tries to nil.

2   **1894 Ireland 3 Wales 0**
     Belfast-born John Lytle's penalty goal gave Ireland their first Triple Crown and championship at the Ulster cricket club in Ballynafeigh.

3   **1948 Ireland 6 Wales 3**
     John Daly from Cobh had his shirt torn by jubilant supporters after Ireland won their first Triple Crown since 1899. Not much was made of the fact that this was also their first Grand Slam.

4   **1964 Ireland 18 England 5**
     Television brought a big rugby event into many homes for the first time.

5   **1982 Ireland 21 Scotland 12**
     A Triple Crown captured on home ground for the first time, with a record six penalties and a drop goal by Ollie Campbell, after Gerry 'Ginger' McLoughlin's try helped them win at Twickenham.

6   **1985 Ireland 13 England 10**
     A late Michael Kiernan drop goal gave Ireland their second Triple Crown in three years.

7   **2000 Ireland 27 France 25**
     Brian O'Driscoll exploded on the scene, scoring three tries in a rare win in Paris, the first in 28 years.

8   **2001 Ireland 20 England 14**
     This was Keith Wood's day as he scored the try that propelled Ireland to one of their most passionate victories.

9   **2007 Ireland 43 England 13**
     Ireland scored four tries in an emotional game at Croke Park, the scene of a crowd massacre by British troops in 1920.

10   **2009 Ireland 17 Wales 15**
     There were dramatic scenes as Ireland captured their first Grand Slam for 61 years by a stroke of fortune. Wales fly-half Stephen Jones's match-saving penalty fell shy of the crossbar.

SHOWJUMPING STORIES

1 ## 1937
A record 43,913 people saw Ireland take a third successive Aga Khan Trophy. The winning team was Ged O'Dwyer on Clontarf, John J. Lewis on Glendalough and Dan Corry on Red Hugh.

2 ## 1937
The Irish horses were late in arriving for the Aachen show, but won the most prestigious Nations Cup on the circuit at the first attempt. Ireland scored 20 Nations Cup wins between 1931 and 1939.

3 ## 1949
Iris Kellett became the first woman to win the Princess Elizabeth Cup.

4 ## 1956
Ireland's showjumping team – Kevin Barry on Ballyneety, Col William Ringrose on Liffey Vale and Patrick Kiernan on Ballynonty – achieved a top-seven finish at the Olympics in Melbourne.

5 ## 1963
Tommy Wade on Dundrum won the King George V Cup.

6 ## 1964
The three-day event team finished fourth at the Tokyo Olympics: Anthony Cameron on Black Salmon, Thomas Brennan on Kilkenny and John Harty on San Michele.

7 ## 1974
Eddie Macken won silver at the World Showjumping Championship on Pele. He won another silver at the 1978 Championship on Boomerang.

8 ## 1979
Ireland's third successive Aga Khan Trophy victory made the team of Paul Darragh, James Kernan, Eddie Macken and Capt. Con Power household names.

9 ## 2000
Cian O'Connor won a short-lived gold medal at the Athens Olympics after his horse tested positive for prohibited substances.

10 ## 2009
Denis Lynch won the prestigious Grand Prix of Aachen title with the gelding Lantinus.

10 SIGNATURE GOLF HOLES

	Course	Hole	Distance
1	Ballybunion	Par-4 2nd	407 m (445 yd)
2	Baltray	Par-4 14th	303.5 m (332 yd)
3	Druids Glen	Par-4 12th	450 m (492 yd)
4	Fota Island	Par-5 18th	457 m (500 yd)
5	Kildare Club Palmer Course	Par-5 7th	554 m (606 yd)
6	Lahinch	Par-4 4th	391.3 m (428 yd)
7	Mount Juliet	Par-4 13th	161 m (176 yd)
8	Portmarnock	Par-4 14th	352 m (385 yd)
9	Royal Portrush	Par-3 14th	192 m (210 yd)
10	Royal County Down	Par-3 4th	208 m (228 yd)

10 GOLFERS

1 **Harry Bradshaw (b. Delgany, Co. Wicklow; 1913–90)**
Bradshaw was second in the 1949 British Open Championship after a tie with Bobby Locke, having famously landed his drive in a broken beer bottle on the fairway at the fifth hole.

2 **Darren Clarke (b. Dungannon, Co. Tyrone; 1968–)**
Second on the European Tour money list in 1998, 2000 and 2003, Clarke defeated Tiger Woods in the final of the 2000 World Match Play Championship.

3 **Fred Daly (b. Portrush, Co. Antrim; 1911–90)**
Daly was the winner of the British Open Championship in 1947 and he won 13 tournaments on the European Tour.

4 **Eamonn Darcy (b. Delgany, Co. Wicklow; 1952–)**
The winner of four European Tour events, Darcy finished second on the Order of Merit in 1976 and third in 1975.

5 **Pádraig Harrington (b. Ballyroan, Co. Laois; 1971–)**
Harrington won the British Open Championship in 2007 and 2008 and the PGA Championship in 2008. He topped the European Order of Merit in 2006.

6 **Paul McGinley (b. Dublin; 1966–)**
Third on the European Tour Order of Merit in 2005, he has won four events on the European Tour. He holed the winning putt for the European team in the 2002 Ryder Cup.

7 **Christy O'Connor Jnr (b. Galway; 1948–)**
The nephew of Christy O'Connor Snr, he participated in the European Tour for 21 seasons. He is famous for one of the best shots in golf history, his 209.3-m (229-yd) two-iron to within 90 cm (3 ft) of the hole in the 1989 Ryder Cup.

8 **Christy O'Connor Snr (b. Knocknacarra, Co. Galway; 1924–)**
The first Irish inductee into the World Golf Hall of Fame, in 2009, he was the winner of 23 events on the European Tour.

9 **Ronan Rafferty (b. Newry, Co. Down; 1964–)**
Rafferty won the European Tour Order of Merit in 1989 and seven European Tour events between 1989 and 1993.

10 **Graeme McDowell (b. Portrush, Co. Antrim, 1979–)**
Winner of the US Open in 2010. He played collegiate golf in the USA rather than the European amateur circuit before turning pro in 2002.

10
MEMBERS OF THE INTERNATIONAL BOXING HALL OF FAME

1   **Jim Braddock (1905–74)**
    Born in Hell's Kitchen, New York, to a Dublin father and Mayo mother, his victory over Max Baer to win the world heavyweight title in 1935 inspired the film the Cinderella Man.

2   **Dan Donnelly (1788–1820)**
    A folk hero thanks to his 1814 prize fight victories against Tom Hall and George Cooper at a spot in the Curragh that became known as Donnelly's Hollow.

3   **Bob Fitzsimmons (1863–1917)**
    Born in England to an Armagh father, he was the first boxer to win titles in three divisions.

4   **Jack Kelly (1862–95)**
    Alias 'Jack Nonpareil Dempsey', Clane-born fighter who won the world middleweight title in 1884 and held it for seven years.

5   **Jack McAuliffe (1866–1937)**
    McAuliffe was a Cork-born lightweight who won the world title in New York in 1886 and held it for six years.

6   **Barry McGuigan (1960–)**
    From Clones, McGuigan won the WBC featherweight title in London on 8 June 1985 and held it for 12 months. McGuigan, his WBC predecessor Eusebio Pedroza and WBA rival Azumah Nelson are all inducted into boxing's Hall of Fame.

7   **Jimmy McLarnin (1907–2004)**
    From Hillsborough, Co Down, the highest-earning boxer prior to the Second World War, he won the world welterweight title in 1933 and regained it from Barney Ross in 1934.

8   **John Morrissey (1831–78)**
    Morrissey from Templemore, Co. Tipperary, was American heavyweight bareknuckle champion in 1958 and the subject of many ballads.

9   **Tom Sharkey (1873–1953)**
    From Dundalk, Co. Louth, Sharkey was defeated in famous 25-round slugging match with James J. Jeffries and boxed in the first world title fight to be filmed. He also won a fight that was refereed by Wyatt Earp.

10 **John L. Sullivan (1858–1918)**
    Born in Boston to an Abbeydorney father and Athlone mother, he was recognized as the first heavyweight champion of gloved boxing in 1881–92.

WORLD BOXING CHAMPIONS

1   **Stephen Collins (b. Cabra; 1964–)**
Collins won the WBO middleweight boxing title in 1994 and WBO super-middleweight title against Chris Eubank in Millstreet in 1995. He defended the title once more against Eubank, twice against Nigel Benn and seven times in all before retiring as champion in 1997.

2   **Bernard Dunne (b. Neilstown; 1980–)**
Winner of the WBA super-bantamweight title against Ricardo Cordoba at the O2 Arena in Dublin in 2009. He held the title for six months.

3   **George Gardner (b. Lisdoonvarna, Co. Clare; 1877–1954)**
The second official holder of the world light-heavyweight title in 1903, Gardner held it for four months.

4   **Eamonn Loughran (b. Ballymena, Co. Antrim; 1970–)**
Winner of the WBO welterweight title in 1994, he defended this title five times until he lost to José Luis Lopez in 1996.

5   **Dave McAuley (b. Larne, Co. Antrim; 1961–)**
McAuley won the IBF world flyweight title in 1989 and defended it five times before losing it in 1992.

6   **Wayne McCullough (b. Belfast; 1970–)**
McCullough won the WBC bantamweight world championship in 1995 in Nagoya, Japan and defended it twice before changing weight.

7   **Mike McTigue (b. Kilnamona, Co. Clare; 1892–1966)**
McTigue won the world light-heavyweight title in the La Scala opera house in civil-war ravaged Dublin in 1923. He held it for two years.

8   **John 'Rinty' Monaghan (b. Belfast; 1918–84)**
Victory over Jackie Patterson in 1948 in his native Belfast made him the undisputed world flyweight champion. He retired undefeated after two defences.

9   **Dave Sullivan (b. Cork; 1877–1929)**
Sullivan won the world featherweight title in 1898 in New York and held it for two years.

10 **Ike O'Neil Weir (b. Lurgan, Co. Armagh; 1867–1908)**
He became the first recognized featherweight world boxing champion, in Indiana in 1889.

OLYMPIC BOXING MEDALLISTS

	Year	Boxer	Weight	Medal
1	1952	John McNally	Bantam	Silver
2	1956	Fred Tiedt	Welter	Silver
3	1956	Johnny Caldwell	Fly	Bronze
4	1956	Freddie Gilroy	Bantam	Bronze
5	1956	Tony Byrne	Light	Bronze
6	1964	Jim McCourt	Light	Bronze
7	1980	Hugh Russell	Fly	Bronze
8	1992	Michael Carruth	Welter	Gold
9	1992	Wayne McCullough	Light Bantam	Silver
10	2008	Paddy Barnes	Light fly	Bronze
=		Ken Egan	Light heavy	Silver
=		Darren Sutherland	Middle	Bronze

This list is a bit of a 'cheat' as there are actually 12 Olympic medallists from Ireland and it didn't seem fair to leave anyone out!

FAMOUS GAA SAGAS

	Year	Winners/Losers	Competition
1	1903	Kerry beat Kildare after 3 matches	All-Ireland football final
2	1925	Roscommon beat Sligo after 6 matches	Connacht football
3	1931	Cork beat Kilkenny after 3 matches	All-Ireland hurling final
4	1941	Carlow beat Wexford after 4 matches	Leinster football
5	1964	Roscommon beat Leitrim after 3 matches	Connacht football
6	1965	Cavan beat Donegal after 3 matches	Ulster football
7	1979	Wexford beat Carlow after 3 matches	Leinster football
8	1991	Meath beat Dublin after 4 matches	Leinster football
9	1997	Meath beat Kildare after 3 matches	Leinster football
10	1998	Offaly beat Clare after 3 matches	All-Ireland hurling semi-final

10 MEMORABLE FOOTBALL SCORES

1 **1903**
Seventeen-year-old Dick Fitzgerald scored a goal that caused the All-Ireland final to be replayed; it led to two more tie-breakers and Kerry's first title against Kildare by 0–8 to 0–2.

2 **1926**
Bill Gorman scored an equalizing goal for Kerry that turned the All-Ireland final into a draw, Kerry 1–3 to Kildare's 0–6; Kerry won the replay.

3 **1933**
Cavan's Vincent McGovern booted the goal that sent four-in-a-row-seeking Kerry out of the semi-final with two minutes to go, Cavan 1–5, Kerry 0–5.

4 **1946**
Two goals in the last three minutes from Kerry's Paddy Burke and Tom Gega O'Connor turned a six-point defeat into a draws in the All-Ireland final, Kerry 2–4, Roscommon 1–7.

5 **1978**
Kerry's Mike Sheehy lofted the ball over Paddy Cullen's head while the Dublin goalkeeper protested a refereeing decision, turning the All-Ireland final into a rout, 5-11 to 0–9.

6 **1982**
Offaly's Seamus Darby snatched the All-Ireland title from Kerry, who were going for five in a row, with two minutes to go, Offaly 1–15, Kerry 0–17.

7 **1983**
Cork's Tadhg Murphy snatched the Munster title from nine-in-a-row-seeking Kerry in the last minute, Cork 3–10, Kerry 3–9.

8 **1991**
Meath's Colm Coyle sent in a speculative ball that bounced and could have gone into the net. However, it bounced over the bar and inspired a four-match series.

9 **1991**
Meath's Kevin Foley ran the length of the field to score the first goal of his career and end a four-match saga against Dublin, Meath 2–11, Dublin 0–15.

10 **2008**
A spectacular solo run goal by Tyrone's Eoin Mulligan in the quarter-final with Dublin helped force a draw, Tyrone 1–14, Dublin 1–14, and quickly accrued a cult following on YouTube. Tyrone won the replay and the All-Ireland title.

MEMORABLE HURLING SCORES 10

1 **1922**
Two goals in the last three minutes from Kilkenny's Paddy Donoghue and Dick Tobin turned a six-point deficit into a win over Tipperary, Kilkenny 4–2, Tipperary 2–6.

2 **1933**
Limerick followers sat up when a young Mick Mackey scored two goals in the first five minutes against Tipperary in the Munster final, Limerick 4–2, Tipperary 1–5.

3 **1939**
On the day that the Second World War broke out, Kilkenny's Terry Leahy whipped over the winning point against Cork from a Paddy Phelan 64-m (70-yd) free, Kilkenny 2–7, Cork 3–3.

4 **1944**
Christy Ring broke through for a solo run goal against Limerick and started building his reputation as the greatest ever, Cork 6–7, Limerick 4–13.

5 **1947**
Kilkenny's Terry Leahy scored the winning point against Cork in a match nominated as the best to date, Kilkenny 0–14, Cork 2–7.

6 **1982**
One of the best points in Croke Park: a 90-m (98½-yd) free by Pat Kirwan gave Offaly a Leinster semi-final victory over Laois, Offaly 3–14, Laois 3–14 and Offaly won the replay.

7 **1991**
Kilkenny's D. J. Carey burst on the scene with a solo run goal against Wexford in the Leinster semi-final, Kilkenny 2–9, Wexford 0–13. He later nominated it as his most important.

8 **1987**
Cork's John Fenton's 50-m (54½-yd) ground stroke against Limerick in the Munster semi-final replay was sublime play, Cork 3–14, Limerick 0–10.

9 **1994**
Offaly's Johnny Dooley ignored instructions to go for a point and goaled a free, predicating a run of 2–4 and victory over Limerick in 'the five-minute final', Offaly 3–16, Limerick 2–13.

10 **1996**
Limerick's Ciaran Carey soloed through for a last-minute winning point against Clare in the Munster semi-final, Limerick 1–13, Clare 0–15.

COUNTIES RANKED BY GAA CLUBS

	County	Number of clubs
1	Cork	260
2	Dublin	215
3=	Limerick	108
=	Antrim	108
5	Wexford	92
6	Galway	88
7	Laois	86
8=	Clare	85
=	Offaly	85
10=	Kerry	82
=	Tipperary	82

Source: Cumann Lúithcleas Gael, Túaraisc don Chomhdháil Bhliantúil 2009

MOST SUCCESSFUL GAA COUNTIES

1 **Kerry**
37 senior, 19 NL*, 10 u-21, 11 minor, 16 junior, 3 SeB*, 11 ladies football

2 **Cork**
36 senior, 19 NL, 22 u-21, 28 minor, 7 interm, 25 junior, 21 camogie, 3 ladies football

3 **Kilkenny**
32 senior, 14 NL, 11 u-21, 19 minor, 2 interm, 9 junior, 12 camogie

4 **Tipperary**
29 senior, 20 NL, 8 u-21, 19 minor, 5 interm, 1 SeB, 12 junior, 5 camogie, 3 ladies football

5 **Dublin**
28 senior, 10 NL, 1 u-21, 14 minor, 9 junior, 26 camogie

6 **Galway**
13 senior, 12 NL, 12 u-21, 14 minor, 2 interm, 6 junior, 1 camogie, 1 ladies football

7 **Wexford**
11 senior, 4 NL, 1 u-21, 3 minor, 4 interm, 3 junior, 4 camogie

8 **Limerick**
9 senior, 11 NL, 4 u-21, 3 minor, 1 interm, 4 junior

9 **Meath**
7 senior, 7 NL, 1 u-21, 3 minor, 1 SeB, 12 junior

10 **Offaly**
7 senior, 2 NL, 1 u-21, 4 minor, 2 junior

* **NL = National League, SeB = Senior B**

PLAYERS WITH THE MOST ALL STAR AWARDS IN HURLING

	Player	Team	Number of awards
1=	D. J. Carey	Kilkenny	9
=	Eddie Keher	Kilkenny	9
=	Henry Shefflin	Kilkenny	9
4=	Noel Skehan	Kilkenny	7
=	Tommy Walsh	Kilkenny	7
6=	Joe McKenna	Limerick	6
=	Nicky English	Tipperary	6
8=	Pat Hartigan	Limerick	5
=	Joe Hennessy	Kilkenny	5
=	Joe Cooney	Galway	5
=	Eoin Kelly	Tipperary	5

There are actually 11 players in this list because of the four-way tie for eighth place.

Eddie Keher won five All Star awards under the current scheme and four Cú Chulainn awards in the 1960s.

SOCCER CLUBS WITH IRISH NAMES

	Club	Location
1	Atlético Vélez Sársfield	Argentina
2	Bloemfontein Celtic	South Africa
3	Celta de Vigo	Spain
4	Celtic	Scotland
5	Deportivo O'Higgins	Chile
6	Dundee Harps (later Dundee United)	Scotland
7	Hibernian	Scotland
8	Hibernians	Malta
9	St. Louis Shamrocks	USA
10	South Carolina Shamrocks	USA

10

REPUBLIC OF IRELAND SOCCER PLAYERS WHO WERE BORN in England

1 John Aldridge

2 Tony Cascarino

3 Kevin Foley

4 Kevin Kilbane

5 Liam Lawrence

6 Mark Lawrenson

7 Mick McCarthy

8 Steven Reid

9 Sean St Ledger

10 Andy Townsend

SOCCER STARS

1   **George Best (b. Belfast; 1946–2005)**
    Soccer's first 'pop star' was the hero of Manchester United's 1968 European Cup win. His descent into alcoholism, which eventually resulted in his death, caused him to retire at 26.

2   **Liam Brady (b. Dublin; 1956–)**
    Brady played for Arsenal from 1973–80. He then became the first Irish player to play in Italy's Serie A, with Juventus, Sampdoria, Inter Milan and Ascori.

3   **Johnny Carey (b. Dublin; 1919–95)**
    Manchester United team captain 1946–53, Carey played for both Irish teams.

4   **Damien Duff (b. Ballyboden, Dublin; 1979–)**
    Ireland's player of the tournament at the 2002 World Cup, he was involved with Chelsea's English Premiership success and their Champions League runs of 2003–6.

5   **Johnny Giles (b. Dublin; 1940–)**
    Most associated with the successful Leeds United team of 1963–75, and he was responsible for reinvigorating the game as player-manager of the Republic of Ireland team until 1981.

6   **Pat Jennings (b. Newry, Co. Down; 1945–)**
    Northern Ireland's most capped player, with 119. He played for Tottenham Hotspur 1964–77 and then Arsenal 1978–85. He played in the 1986 World Cup at the age of 41.

7   **Roy Keane (b. Cork; 1971–)**
    Keane was instrumental in securing Manchester United's Champions League final place in 1999 (although he was suspended for the final itself). He controversially stormed out of the Irish training camp prior to the 2002 World Cup.

8   **Paul McGrath (b. Dublin; 1959–)**
    A Manchester United and Aston Villa player, he had a cult following through his 83 performances for Ireland, including one European Championship and two World Cups.

9   **David O'Leary (b. Dublin; 1958–)**
    An Arsenal player from 1975 to 1993. He won 68 caps for his national side and scored the winning penalty to put them through to the 1990 World Cup quarter-finals.

10 **Liam Whelan (b. Cabra, Dublin; 1935–58)**
    Having made 98 first-team appearances, at the age of 22 he was one of the eight Manchester United players who were killed in the Munich Air Disaster.

GREAT YEARS FOR THE IFA

1   **1882**
The Irish team competed for the first time in a soccer international, making Ireland the fourth of the 208 national soccer teams to take the field.

2   **1914**
Ireland won the British Home Championship, beating England 3–0 away and drawing with Scotland in front of 27,000 spectators in Belfast.

3   **1919**
A visit from the English team to soccer-starved Belfast attracted Ireland's first 40,000 attendance.

4   **1957**
Northern Ireland beat England 3–2 at Wembley to share the British Home Championship.

5   **1958**
Northern Ireland qualified for the quarter-finals of the World Cup by beating Italy in a qualifying play-off.

6   **1982**
Gerry Armstrong's goal meant Northern Ireland beat hosts Spain in the World Cup to qualify for the last 12.

7   **1983**
Norman Whiteside's goal inflicted West Germany's first ever home defeat in a European qualifier in Hamburg.

8   **1986**
The Northern Ireland team qualified for the World Cup finals.

9   **2005**
David Healy's goal gave Northern Ireland a 1–0 victory over England in a World Cup qualifier.

10   **2006**
David Healy's hat-trick gave Northern Ireland a 3–2 win over Spain in a European Championship qualifier in Belfast.

The IFA, founded in 1880, selected players from the 32 counties until 1950 when it joined FIFA. Since 1954 its teams have played as Northern Ireland.

GREAT YEARS FOR THE FAI

10

1 **1924**
Ireland reached the quarter-finals of the most important international soccer competition prior to the foundation of the World Cup – the Olympic Games – only to lose 3–2 to the Netherlands after extra time.

2 **1949**
England's first home defeat to a non-British team was to Ireland, by 2–0 at Goodison Park.

3 **1963**
Ireland qualified for the quarter-finals of the European Championship for the first time, defeating Austria 3–2 in chaotic scenes at Dalymount Park.

4 **1984**
The national youth soccer team finished fourth at the World Cup in Moscow.

5 **1988**
Ireland qualified for the last eight of the European Championship.

6 **1990**
Ireland qualified for the quarter-finals of the World Cup.

7 **1994**
Ireland qualified for the round of 16 in the World Cup by beating eventual finalists Italy 1–0 at the Giants Stadium.

8 **1996**
The national side won both the European Under-16 and Under-18 Championships under charismatic manager Brian Kerr.

9 **2002**
Ireland qualified for the World Cup round of 16.

10 **2010**
In a controversial match, Ireland narrowly missed out on a place at the World Cup finals, losing 2–1 on aggregate to France in a play-off after Thierry Henry handled the ball in the run-up to the winning goal.

The FAI, founded in 1922 after a Dublin club was asked to replay a cup semi-final in Belfast, selected players from all 32 counties for matches against other FIFA members until 1950. Since 1954 it has played as the Republic of Ireland and since 1964 it has been entitled to select all Irish passport holders.

MOST-CAPPED REPUBLIC OF IRELAND PLAYERS

	Player	Dates	Caps*
1=	Steve Staunton	1988–2002	102
=	Shay Given	1996–	102
=	Kevin Kilbane	1997–	102
4	Robbie Keane	1998–	96
5	Niall Quinn	1986–2002	91
6	Tony Cascarino	1985–99	88
7	Paul McGrath	1985–97	83
8=	Packie Bonner	1981–96	80
=	Damien Duff	1998–	80
10	Ray Houghton	1986–97	73

* Figures up to the end of 2009

MOST-CAPPED NORTHERN IRELAND PLAYERS

	Player	Dates	Caps*
1	Pat Jennings	1964–86	119
2	Mal Donaghy	1980–94	91
3	Sammy McIlroy	1972–87	88
4	Keith Gillespie	1995–2008	86
5	Maik Taylor	1999–	80
6	David Healy	2000–	77
7	Jimmy Nicholl	1976–86	73
8=	Michael Hughes	1992–2004	71
=	Aaron Hughes	1998–	71
10	David McCreery	1976–90	67

* Figures up to the end of 2009

SOCCER CLUBS IN EUROPE

1   **1966**
    Shamrock Rovers drew 1–1 with Bayern Munich in Dublin and lost 3–2 in Munich in the European Cup Winners' Cup.

2   **1967**
    Linfield beat Luxembourg and Norwegian opposition to reach the quarter-finals of the European Cup, drawing 2–2 with CSKA Sofia at home and losing 1–0 away.

3   **1974**
    Glentoran beat Romanian and Norwegian opposition to reach the quarter-finals of the European Cup Winners' Cup, losing 2–0 and 5–0 to Borussia Moenchengladbach.

4   **1975**
    Athlone drew 0–0 with AC Milan in the UEFA Cup in St Mel's Park and lost 3–0 in the San Siro.

5   **1979**
    Dundalk drew with Glasgow Celtic 0–0 at home in the European Cup and lost 3–2 in Parkhead.

6   **1984**
    In the UEFA Cup, Bohemians defeated Glasgow Rangers 3–2 in Dalymount but lost 2–0 in Ibrox.

7   **1991**
    Cork City drew 1–1 with Bayern in Cork in the UEFA Cup but lost 2–0 in Munich.

8   **2000**
    Bohemians defeated Aberdeen on away goals in the UEFA Cup, winning 2–1 in Pittodrie but losing 1–0 in Dublin.

9   **2004**
    Shelbourne defeated Hadjuk Split to go within a match of the Champions League group stages. They drew 0–0 with Deportivo La Coruña at home, only to lose 3–0 in Spain.

10 **2008**
    St Patrick's Athletic went within a match of the UEFA Cup group stages drawing with Hertha Berlin 0–0 at home but losing 2–0 away.

FOREIGN INTERNATIONALS WHO PLAYED IN THE IRISH SOCCER LEAGUES

	Player	Irish club(s)	International team
1	Jason Batty	Bohemians	New Zealand
2	Romuald Boco	Sligo Rovers	Benin
3	David Atiba Charles	Glenavon	Trinidad & Tobago
4	Wesley Charles	Sligo Rovers/Bray/Galway	St Vincent & the Grenadines
5	Jeff Clarke	St Patrick's Athletic/Langford	Canada
6	Dominic Iorfa	Cork/Waterford	Nigeria
7	Kupono Low	Sligo Rovers	USA
8	Shaun Lowther	UCD	Canada
9	Joseph Ndo	Bohemians/Shamrock Rovers/Shelbourne/St Patrick's Athletic	Cameroon
10	Fitzroy Simpson	Linfield	Jamaica

10 GOALKEEPERS WHO HAVE SCORED GOALS

Player

1 **John Commins**

Hurling goalkeeper who became the first to score a goal in the All-Ireland final as Galway lost to Cork, in the under-21 final.

2 **Alan Fettis**

Scored twice for Hull City soccer team during a striker injury crisis.

3 **David Fitzgerald**

Clare goalkeeper, scorer of the match-winning penalty in the 1995 Munster hurling final and a dramatic last-minute equalizer from a penalty in the 1999 Munster hurling semi-final against Tipperary.

4 **Damien Fitzhenry**

Wexford goalkeeper scored two goals in the 2001 All-Ireland hurling quarter-final against Limerick, and another in the 2007 quarter-final against Tipperary.

5 **John Hevey**

Scored direct from play for Shelbourne against Waterford at Kilcohan Park in 1971.

6 **Pat Jennings**

Newry-born soccer goalkeeper sent a kick out into the Manchester United goal during the 1967 Charity Shield match at Old Trafford.

7 **Alan Mannus**

Scored for Linfield in 2003 with a goalkick against Omagh Town.

8 **Marian McCarthy**

Scored a goal direct from a puckout in the 1985 All-Ireland camogie semi-final.

9 **Niall Quinn**

During a match between Manchester City and Derby County in 1991, the Manchester City goalkeeper was sent off and Niall Quinn went in goal. He scored and saved a penalty in the same match.

10 **Peter Reilly**

Drumcondra-born goalkeeper whose penchant for bringing the ball in his hands to the halfway line, then dribbling through and scoring, forced a change in the rules in 1910.

HOCKEY MILESTONES

	Year	Team	Achievement
1	1908	Men	Olympic silver medal
2	1948	Men	Triple Crown
3	1950	Women	Triple Crown
4	1972	Men	Won Santander Tournament
5	1977	Men	Intercontinental Cup runners-up
6	1978	Men	Qualified for World Cup for first time
7	1983	Women	Won Intercontinental Cup
8	1994	Women	Hosted World Cup, finished 11th
9	1997	Men	Fifth at European Hockey Championships
10	2005	Men	Won Euro Nations Championship

Ireland have qualified for the women's hockey World Cup finals three times and twice for the men's.

GREAT YEARS FOR CRICKET

1   **1902**
    The Irish, captained by Tim O'Brien, played against a London County side including
    W. G. Grace. The Irish won convincingly by 238 runs.

2   **1904**
    Ireland's first victory against a Test-playing nation came when they defeated South Africa.

3   **1928**
    Ireland played their first match against the West Indies and won by 60 runs.

4   **1969**
    One of Ireland's most famous victories to date came in a one-day international against a
    West Indian side including Clive Lloyd and Clyde Walcott at Sion Mills in County Tyrone.
    The Irish won by nine wickets after bowling their opponents out for 25.

5   **1979**
    A morale-boosting draw with Sri Lanka in a rain-hit first-class match, Ireland scored a
    total of 341/7 in two innings while Sri Lanka made 288/6 in one innings.

6   **2003**
    Ireland beat Zimbabwe by ten wickets, ten years after joining the ICC as an associate
    member in 1993.

7   **2007**
    A draw with Zimbabwe was achieved thanks primarily to Ireland's first ever World Cup
    century by man-of-the-match Jeremy Bray and economical bowling in the final overs by
    Trent Johnston and Andre Botha.

8   **2007**
    Ireland's most prestigious victory came when they beat the fourth-ranked team in the
    world, Pakistan, by three wickets in their second World Cup match. These two results were
    sufficient to advance Ireland to the 'Super 8' stage of the tournament.

9   **2007**
    The Irish team scored a 74-run victory over Test-playing nation Bangladesh, the team
    ranked ninth in the world.

10 **2009**
    Another victory over Bangladesh meant that the Irish progressed to the second round of
    the ICC Twenty20 World Cup.

MEN WHO PLAYED MORE THAN ONE SPORT FOR IRELAND

Name	Sports
1 Oscar Andrews	Cricket/hockey
2 Jack Bowden	Cricket/hockey
3 Brian Carney	Rugby League/Rugby Union
4 Noel Cantwell	Cricket/soccer
5 Bud Hamilton	Badminton/cricket/hockey/tennis
6 Willoughby Hamilton	Amateur soccer/badminton/tennis
7 Kevin O'Flanagan	Rugby/soccer
8 Mick O'Flanagan	Rugby/soccer
9 James Parke	Golf/Rugby/tennis
10 Frank Stoker	Rugby/tennis

Kevin and Mick O'Flanagan were brothers.

ACKNOWLEDGEMENTS

Associated Press/Daily Mail
British Biographical Archive
Thomas Broderick
Cambridge University Press
Central Statistics Office
Cumann Camógaíochta
Cumann Luthchleas Gael
Cumann Peil Gael na mBan
Daft.ie
Dictionary of Irish Biography,
Sean Donnelly
Seamus Dooley
Dublin Airport Authority
Examiner Newspapers
Fáilte Ireland
Football Association of Ireland
GAA Museum
An Garda Siochana
Claire Grady
Gill & MacMillan
Harper Collins Ireland
Health Service Executive
History Ireland
Horse Racing Ireland
House of Commons Parliamentary Papers
(Westminster)
Houses of the Oireachtas archive
Independent Newspapers
Institute of Public Administration
Irish Amateur Archery Association
Irish Amateur Boxing Association
Irish Congress of Trade Unions
Irish Football Association
Irish Hockey Association
Irish News
Irish Newspaper Archives
Irish Permanent House Price Index
Irish Press
Irish Rugby Football Union
Irish Times
Irish Tour Operators Federation
Irish Travel Agents Association

JSTOR Arts and Sciences Collections
electronic resource
Graeme Linehan
Arthur Mattews
Dónal McAnallen
Brendan McWilliams
Damien Mooney
Siobhan Moore
Mary Moran
National Archives
National Library of Ireland
National Micromedia
National Museum of Ireland
Neilsen
Northern Ireland Statistics and Research
Agency
Northern Ireland Tourist Board
David O'Neill
Ordnance Survey of Ireland
Oxford Dictionary of National Biography
Oxford University Press
Paddy Power Bookmakers
Proquest
Public Records Office of Northern
Ireland
Raidió Telefís Éireann library services
Claire Rourke
Royal Dublin Society
Royal Institute of the Architects of Ireland
Royal Irish Academy
St Patrick's College Maynooth library
KG Saur biographical archive online
Peter Sherrard
Ger Siggins
Thomson Gale
Tourism Ireland
Trinity College Dublin library services
UCD library
Ulster Museum
Ulster Newsletter
Fintan Vallely
HW Wilson Biography Index